PICCOLO ENCYCLOP
OF USEFUL FACTS
Revised Edition with a new Sports section

JEAN STROUD

Cover Illustration by Brian Webb
Text Illustrations by Robin Lawrie

A Piccolo Original Pan Books London and Sydney

First published 1973 by Pan Books Ltd,
Cavaye Place, London SW10 9PG
Reprinted 1973 (twice)
Revised editions published 1974, 1975
This revised edition published 1977
© Jean Stroud 1973, 1974, 1975, 1977
ISBN 0 330 25207 0

Printed in Great Britain by
Cox & Wyman Ltd, London, Reading and Fakenham

CONTENTS

1 THE SOLAR SYSTEM

The Solar System

The centre of the Solar System is the Sun. The Sun is one of the millions of stars that make up the Universe. The Earth is one of nine major planets which revolve round the Sun, bound to it by the force of gravity. The Sun, the planets, their satellites and a large number of other lesser bodies including comets and asteroids as well as interplanetary dust and gas form the Solar System. The origin of the Solar System is not known; it is thought that its age must be at least 5,000 million years.

The Galaxy

The Galaxy, more popularly known as the Milky Way, is a mass of stars. It is a glowing band of light seen on dark nights stretching around the sky along the line of the galactic equator. Galileo discovered that The Milky Way consists of an enormous number of faint stars. They are whirling about in space. The Milky Way is, in fact, the visible sign of the Galaxy.

The Milky Way system (the Galaxy or Galactic system) is a huge star system of which the Sun is a member. The diameter of the Galaxy is about 100,000 light-years. The maximum thickness is about 20,000 light-years. The Sun lies about 25,000 light-years from the centre. The Galaxy rotates round its centre – the Sun takes about 225,000,000 years to complete one revolution known, unofficially, as a 'cosmic year'.

There are about 1,000 million galaxies similar to the Milky Way, each made up of thousands of millions of stars, dust and gas, and only three are visible to the naked eye. These are the Andromeda Spiral (which closely resembles ours in shape, size and number of stars) in the northern hemisphere, and the two Nebulae of Magellanic clouds in the far south.

Galaxies are units of the Universe in the same way as atoms are units of matter. They are of various shapes. The nearest galaxy is about two million light-years away from Earth.

The Sun

Age	At least 6,000 million years old
Diameter	865,000 miles
Surface Area	12,000 times that of Earth
Temperature	Surface: About 6,000°C Internal: About 35,000,000°C
Distance from the Earth	92,868,000 miles
Volume	1,300,000 (Earth=1)
Mass	330,000 (Earth=1)
Density	0·25 (Earth=1)
Force of Gravity on the Surface	27·7 (Earth=1)
Period of Rotation on its Axis	25·38 days
Speed of Rotation at its Equator	4,407 mph

The Moon

Diameter	2,158 miles
Surface Area	14,660,000 sq. miles
Temperature (on lunar equator)	Day: estimated +220°F Night: estimated −250°F
Distance from the Earth	Maximum: 252,700 miles Minimum: 221,460 miles
Volume	0·0203 that of the Earth
Mass	1/81·3 of that of the Earth (=0·0123)
Density	3·3 (water=1); 0·06 (Earth=1)
Speed in Orbit	2,287 mph (0·63 miles per second)
Time of Revolution	27 days, 7 hours, 43 minutes
Synodic Period (Interval between one new Moon and the next)	approx 29·5 days

Note: To convert Fahrenheit to Centigrade see p. 63.

The Planets

Planet	Distance from the Earth Maximum (in miles)	Minimum (in miles)	Distance from the Sun (in miles)	Period of Revolution Round the Sun	Equatorial Diameter (in miles)	Maximum Surface Temperature (F)	Number of Satellites	Surface Gravity (Earth = 1)
Mercury	136,900,000	49,100,000	36,000,000	88 days	2,900	+770?	0	0·37
Venus	160,900,000	25,700,000	67,200,000	224·7 days	7,700	+800?	0	0·89
Earth	—	—	92,868,000	365·3 days	7,927	+140	1	1·00
Mars	247,000,000	34,000,000	141,500,000	687 days	4,219	+80	2	0·39
Jupiter	597,000,000	362,000,000	483,300,000	11·9 years	88,700	−200	12	2·54
Saturn	1,023,000,000	773,000,000	886,100,000	29·5 years	75,100	−240	9	1·13
Uranus	1,946,000,000	1,594,000,000	1,783,000,000	84·0 years	29,300	−310	5	1·09
Neptune	2,891,000,000	2,654,000,000	2,793,000,000	164·8 years	27,700	−360	2	1·41
Pluto	4,506,000,000	2,605,000,000	3,666,000,000	248·4 years	±9,000?	?	0	?

The Constellations

A Constellation is a group of stars within a definite region of the sky. The word means 'star groups'. For as long as man has existed on this planet, the positions of the stars have remained virtually unchanged and by knowing the positions of the constellations it is possible to locate stars, planets, comets and meteors. For thousands of years man has used his knowledge of the constellations to guide himself from place to place during journeys over the surface of the earth. On a cloudless night between 2,000 and 3,000 stars are visible to the naked eye. With the aid of a great astronomical telescope, like the one on Mount Wilson in California, something like 50,000,000 stars can be seen.

The largest constellation is *Hydra* (the Sea Serpent) which contains at least 68 stars visible to the naked eye. The smallest constellation is *Crux Australis* (Southern Cross).

The following constellations are the most important ones in the northern hemisphere:

Scientific Name	*English Name*
Andromeda	The Chained Lady
Auriga	The Charioteer
Bootes	The Herdsman
Canis major	The Greater Dog
Canis minor	The Smaller Dog
Cassiopeia	The wife of Cephus
Cygnus	The Swan
Gemini	The Twins
Leo	The Lion
Lyra	The Lyre or Harp
Pegasus	The Winged Horse
Perseus	The Legendary Hero
Sagittarius	The Archer
Scorpius	The Scorpion
Taurus	The Bull
Ursa major	The Great Bear
Ursa minor	The Little Bear

The Stars

Any celestial body, whether fixed or planetary, is called a star. A star is a heavenly body that shines with its own light, produced by substances raised to a high temperature.

The stars are classed according to their brightness as seen from the Earth. The unit of brightness is called the *magnitude*. Magnitude 0 is the brightest. Stars as faint as the sixth magnitude can be seen by the unaided eye. Except our own Sun, the nearest star is the Proxima Centauri which is 4·3 light years (40×10^{12} km) away.

The Twenty Brightest Stars

Star	Magnitude	Star	Magnitude
Sirius	−1·58	Agena	0·66
Canopus	−0·73	Altair	0·80
Rigil Kentaurus	−0·27	Aldebaran	0·85
Arcturus	−0·06	Acrux	0·87
Vega	0·04	Antares	0·98
Capella	0·09	Spica	1·00
Rigel	0·15	Fomalhaut	1·16
Procyon	0·37	Pollux	1·16
Achernar	0·53	Deneb	1·26
Betelgeuse	0·90	Beta Crucis	1·31

Glossary of Astronomical Terms

Atmosphere – The gaseous mantle surrounding a planet or other body.

Black Body Radiation – A theoretical body which completely absorbs all radiation reaching its surface and reflects none – thus appearing quite black.

Celestial Sphere – The imaginary sphere, concentric with the observer, on which the stars appear to be fixed.

Circumpolar Stars – Those which can never set, because their distance from the celestial pole is less than the distance of the pole from the horizon at the place of observation.

Conjunction – Apparent closeness of two heavenly bodies.

Corona – The outermost region of the Sun's atmosphere.

Cosmic Rays – High-energy particles reaching the Earth from outer space.

Cosmogony – Study of the origin and development of the universe or of any particular part of it.

Cosmology – Study of the universe as a whole, its general nature and structure.

Craters (Lunar) – Circular formations of all sizes that are a prominent feature of the Moon.

Ecliptic – The path that the centre of the Sun's disc traces out on the celestial sphere. Also the projection of the Earth's orbital plane on the celestial sphere.

Light, Speed of – 186,000 miles per second.

Light-Year – The distance travelled by light in one year – just under 6,000,000,000,000 miles.

Magnitude (visual) – The unit of brightness of a star. A star of the first magnitude is said to be 100 times brighter than one of the sixth magnitude.

Meteor – A small particle of rock or metal ore hurtling through space. When meteors enter the Earth's gravitational field they look like 'shooting stars'.

Milky Way – The luminous band seen in the night sky, made up of large numbers of faint stars.

Novae – Individual faint stars that suddenly brighten to a brilliant maximum, then fade again.

Occultation – The covering up of one celestial body by another. An eclipse is, strictly speaking, an occultation of the Sun by the Moon.

Parsec – A measure of distance. A parsec is 3·26 light years (approx. 19,000,000,000,000 miles).

Poles, Celestial – The two points where the Earth's axis intersects the celestial sphere.

Pulsar – One theory is that it is a rotating neutron star of immense density. The discovery of the first pulsar (or pulsating radio source) was in 1968.

Pulsating (or expanding) Universe – A model universe of galaxies in which expansion takes place so that the distance between galaxies constantly increases.

Quasars – Popular name for quasi-stellar objects. Mysterious objects which appear as sources of strong radio frequency radiations. They are seen as small star-like objects on photographs, and their existence was established in 1962.

Red Shift – The phenomenon in which the spectral lines of galaxies are shifted towards the red end of the spectrum. The red shift indicates that the galaxies are receding.

Scintillation – The official term for 'twinkling'.

Specific Gravity – The density of any substance, compared with that of an equal volume of water.

Spectroscope – An instrument for the analysis of light.

Sun-Spot – One of the numerous dark patches which may be seen on the Sun's surface.

Supernovae – Extremely luminous novae. Only three supernovae have been identified in our own Galaxy, the brightest on record being in the constellation Cassiopeia, which reached an apparent magnitude of −3·5.

Zenith – Point of heavens directly above the observer.

2 HOW LIFE BEGAN

How Life Began

More than a million different kinds of animal inhabit the earth. But no one really knows how life began. It probably began about 1,000 million years ago in some ancient sea. Some scientists believe that chemicals in the sea and air combined to form organic compounds, that these joined together and developed the characteristics of life.

The first speck of life must have been very simple – it may have been somewhat similar to the viruses we know today – but, most important, it was able to reproduce. Life evolved over millions of years – and changes are still taking place today.

Era	Period	Important Geological Past	Millions of years ago
PALAEOZOIC (Age of Ancient Life)	Cambrian	Mild climates. Invertebrates only – jellyfish, starfish, worms and sponges. No land animals.	550
	Ordovician	Flooding of continents. Very powerful earth movements. First vertebrates appear, known as *Ostracoderms*.	445

Silurian

Warm climate. Coral reefs develop. Spiders and scorpions become first air-breathers. Invertebrates widespread. First land plants appear but are still leafless.　375

Devonian

'The Age of Fish' – ancestors of all modern fish evolve. Amphibians appear. Plants with roots, stems and leaves evolve. Ferns, seed-ferns and horsetails develop. Millipedes, mites and wingless insects appear.　350

Carboniferous

Insects now common. First reptile-like creatures appear. Amphibia develop quickly in warm, moist, coal forests. Giant evergreens flourish.　250

Permian

Varied climate. Mountains form. Primitive reptiles become more common. Modern insects such as cicadas and true beetles develop.　230

MESOZOIC (Age of Reptiles)

Triassic

Widespread desert conditions. First mammals. First ichthyosaurs (carnivorous, fish-shaped reptiles) evolve. Early meat-eating dinosaurs appear. Procompsognathus and Saltoposuchus are common, as is the plant-eating Plateosaurus.　200

Jurassic

Lands swampy. The first true bird, Archaeopteryx, appears. Ichthyosaurs, reptiles that were completely adapted to life in the sea, surface to take air into their lungs. The Age of Dinosaurs: Megalosaurus, the first dinosaur to be named, and giants like Brachiosaurus, Diplodocus and Brontosaurus – and an early armoured dinosaur, Stegosaurus.   165

Cretaceous

Cool climates. Major mountain building – Rocky Mountains and Andes begin to emerge. Flowering plants and bees are new in the world. Primitive birds, Ichthyornis and Hesperornis, and the first snakes appear. Fish, similar to those we know today – herring, swordfish, sturgeon, pike, sharks – swim in the seas. The old dinosaurs have vanished. New armoured dinosaurs, Ankylosaurus, are seen. Duck-billed dinosaurs, Iguanodon, Trachodon, Corythosaurus and Parasaurolophus – live near water. Psittacosaurus (parrot lizard), and the horned dinosaurs, the last of the great dinosaur families – Protoceratops, Triceratops, Monoclonius and Styracosaurus – roam the land. Tyrannosaurus, the largest flesh-eating animal of all, walks the earth. Pterosaurs (flying reptiles) widespread.   130

CAINOZOIC **Palaeocene**
(The Age **and Eocene**
of Mammals)

Generally hot. Mountain ranges continue to grow. Rise of placental mammals (whose young are nourished directly by the mother's blood until birth). Ancestors of the elephant, rhinoceros, horse, pig and cow come into existence. Crocodiles, turtles and land tortoises evolve and all groups of insects we know today. Primitive monkeys and gibbons appear. Flowering plants widespread.

65

Oligocene

Land mass grows at the expense of the sea. Warm climate. Forests get smaller, grasslands spread and plant-eating animals increase – small elephants with short trunks and tusks in upper and lower jaws, giant rhinoceroses. New species of crabs, snails and sea-urchins evolve, as do ancestors of modern cats, dogs and bears. A primitive ape, possibly related to the ancestors of man, appears.

36

Miocene

Climate mild. Europe and Asian land masses finally join. Primitive manlike ape, Proconsul, spread from Africa to Asia and Europe. A gibbon-like ape, Pliopithecus, common in forests of southern Europe. Elephants steadily increasing in size, spread from Africa into Europe, Asia and North

America. Long-legged water birds, ducks and pelicans in rivers and lakes. Primitive penguins live in Antarctica.

26

Pliocene

Continents and oceans begin to take roughly their present shape. Climates cooling. Marine life – both plant and animal – much as it is today. Elephants, horses, other mammals more like modern types. Man-like apes continue to develop, not only the forest-dwellers but the species known as Australopithecus, which walk in open country and may be ancestral to man.

11

Pleistocene

Succeeding Ice Ages leave only harder varieties of plants in Europe – oak, willow, poplar, elm, hawthorn. Stone Age cave men. Mammoths and gigantic mammals.

1

Holocene

Ice-sheets disappear. (The Ice Age may not yet be over – we may be living in an inter-glacial, in which case the cold will return.) Britain is cut off from the Continent. Modern mammals and man dominant.

0·1

Some Extinct Animals

1. PREHISTORIC ANIMALS (which lived long before Man appeared on earth):

Coelacanth	(primitive fish) – lived 300 million years ago. It was presumed to have been extinct around 70 million years ago, yet specimens have been caught recently.
Meganeura	A giant insect with a wing span of up to 30 inches – similar to a dragonfly.
Pteranodon	Giant flying reptile with wing span of up to 25 feet.
Diplodocus	The 'long tailed' herbivorous dinosaur which lived in the United States and grew up to lengths in excess of 90 feet.
Iguanodon	This dinosaur (the term, derived from the Greek, means 'terrible lizard'), from the Early Cretaceous period reached about 15 feet in height when standing. Remains have been found on the Isle of Wight.
Tyrannosaurus	Literally 'tyrant lizard' and most famous of all the carnivorous reptiles. They had short, weak fore-limbs and strong hind limbs and tails.
Moa	A huge flightless bird from New Zealand resembling vaguely ostriches and emus, except that the moas were perhaps three or four times larger.
Baluchitherium	Related to present-day rhinos, this huge mammal lived in Baluchistan and Mongolia and measured 18 feet at the shoulder.
Megatherium	Giant ground sloth – remains found in South America.

Other prehistoric animals were: Eusthenopteron, Ichthyostega, Eryops, Gerrothorax, Diplocaulus, Seymouria, Stenaulorhynchus, Mosasaurus, Mandasuchus, Plateosaurus, Cetiosaurus, Coelophysis, Ornithomimus, Deinonychus, Scelidosaurus, Polacanthus, Hypsilophodon, Corythosaurus, Rhamphorhynchus, Phororhacos, Aepyornis, Cryptoclidus, Tanystropheus, Dimetrodon, Lystrosaurus, Cynognathus, Megazostrodon, Diprotodon, Sivatherium, Hyracotherium, Coelondonta, Deinotherium, Glyptodon.

2. Species that have become extinct since the age of Man – ie, in the last 200,000 years:

Heath Hen (*Tympanuchus cupido cupido*) An extinct North American grouse which inhabited wooded districts. The last to survive was seen on the island of Martha's Vineyard, Massachusetts, in the early 1930s.

Passenger Pigeon (*Ectopistes migratorius*) North American bird which nested in great colonies and wheeled in flocks dense enough to darken the sky. The last of the species, a bird hatched in captivity, died in the Cincinnati (Ohio) Zoo in 1914.

Dodo The common name for two extinct species of large, clumsy, flightless birds which inhabited the islands of Mauritius and Réunion in the Indian Ocean. The Mauritius dodo (*Raphus cucullatus*) was slightly larger than a turkey. The dodo has been extinct since about 1680.

Great Auk (*Pinguinus impennis*) A large flightless sea bird, slightly smaller than a tame goose. The body was 30 inches long, the wings used in swimming under water being less than 6 inches long. It bred at St Kilda, the Faeroe Islands, Iceland and Funk Island off Newfoundland. The last reported sightings were in the early 1850s.

Quagga (*Equus quagga*) A zebra-like animal formerly found in vast herds on the great plains of South Africa. The last died in the London Zoo in 1872.

Steller's Sea Cow (*Hydro-damalis stelleri*) Reached a length of about 24 feet, with a relatively small head and broad, horizontal forked tail fluke. They browsed on the seaweed in the bays of the Bering and Copper Islands in the Bering Strait near Kamchatka. Less than thirty years after its discovery in 1741 by Georg W. Steller the animal was exterminated.

Aurochs (*Bos taurus primi-genius*) The wild ox of Europe from which domestic cattle are descended. It survived in the Jaktorow forest of central Poland until 1627. It was 6 feet high at the shoulder, black in colour, with spreading, forwardly curved horns.

Mammoth Broadly speaking, any extinct member of the elephant subfamily *Elephantinae*. Similar to living elephants in the body skeleton, mammoths differ from them, and each other, in the shape of the skull, tusk form and molar structure. One of the most complete mammoth carcasses was that unearthed in 1899 from the bed of a river in Siberia.

Sabre-toothed Tiger
(*Smilodon*) A large, short-limbed carnivore with immense canine teeth. Among living cats, only the lion approaches Smilodon in massiveness and even the largest lions do not reach the proportions of the largest sabre-tooths, which ranged in the Pleistocene period in North and South America. It became extinct not more than a few thousand years ago.

3 THE WORLD WE LIVE IN

The Earth

Total Surface Area (estimated)	196,836,000 sq. miles
Land Area	55,786,000 sq. miles
Water Area	141,050,000 sq. miles
Equatorial Circumference	24,901·8 miles
Equatorial Diameter	7,926·5 miles
Polar Diameter	7,900 miles
Centre of the Earth	Almost 4,000 miles beneath our feet
Density	5·52
Atmosphere	77·6 per cent nitrogen; 20·7 per cent oxygen
Temperature	Exceeds 4,000°F at the core
Weight (estimated)	5,882,000,000,000,000,000,000 tons
Age (estimated)	4,700 million years
Mean Orbital Speed	185 miles per second (66,000 mph) or 584,000,000 miles in a year
Mean Distance to the Sun	92,870,000 miles
Mean Distance to the Moon	238,854 miles

It is estimated that the Earth attracts 14·9 tons of cosmic dust annually.

The Hottest Place on Earth	Dallol, Ethiopia, where the annual average temperature is 34·4°C (94° F).
The Coldest Place on Earth	The Pole of Cold, in Antarctica, which has an annual average temperature of −72°F, 16°F lower than the Pole.

Highest Rainfall	73·62 in. fell in 24 hours at Cilaos, Réunion, Indian Ocean on March 15th–16th, 1952. This is equal to 7,435 tons of rain per acre.
Most Rainy Days (Year)	Bahia Felix, Chile had 348 rainy days in 1916 (annual average 325 days).
Longest Drought	c. 400 years to 1971, Desierto de Atacama, Chile.
Greatest Snowfall (Year)	1,224·5 in. (31,102 mm) Paradise, Mt Rainier, Washington, USA, February 19th, 1971 – February 18th, 1972.
Highest Shade Temperature	136·4°F: Al' Aziziyah, Libya, recorded on September 13th, 1922.
Lowest Screen Temperature	—126·9°F: Vostok, Antarctica, on August 24th, 1960.
London	has had 7 'White' Christmas days since 1900: in 1906, 1917, 1923, 1927, 1938, 1956 and 1970.

The Continents

The Continents are the main land masses of the globe.

	Area (sq. km)
Europe	4,929,000
Asia	27,611,000
USSR	22,402,000
Africa	30,258,000
America	42,063,000
Oceania (Australia, New Zealand, New Guinea and the Islands of the Pacific)	8,510,000

Main Oceans

	Area of basin (in sq. miles)	Greatest depth (in feet)	Name of deepest area
Pacific	64,186,300	36,198	Mariana Trench
Atlantic	31,814,640	30,246	Puerto Rico Trench
Indian	28,350,500	24,442	Sunda Trench
Arctic	5,427,000	17,880	Eurasia Basin

Land Below Sea Level

Lowest point	Approx. depth below sea level (in feet)
Dead Sea (Israel-Jordan)	1,296
Qattara Depression (Libyan Desert, Egypt)	436
Death Valley (California)	282
Lake Eyre (South Australia)	52
Netherlands coastal areas	15

The World's Highest Mountains

Peak	Country	Height (in feet)
EUROPE		
ALPS. The highest peaks are:		
Mont Blanc		15,771
Monte Rosa		15,203
Dom		14,913
Matterhorn		14,690
Jungfrau		13,642
Eiger		13,025

ASIA

Everest	Nepal-Tibet	29,028
Godwin Austen (K2)	Kashmir	28,250
Kanchenjunga	Nepal-India	28,208
Nanga Parbat	Kashmir	26,660
Annapurna	Nepal	26,504
Nanda Devi	India	25,645
Kungur	Sinkiang	25,325
Minya Konka	China	24,900

USSR

Communism Peak	USSR (Pamir range of Central Asia)	24,590
Mount Elbruz	Caucasus Range	18,526
Koshtan Tau	Caucasus Range	17,096

AFRICA

Kilimanjaro	Tanzania	19,340
Kenya	Kenya	17,058
Margherita	Uganda – Republic of Congo	16,763
Ras Dashan	Ethiopia	15,158

AMERICA (South)

Aconcagua	Argentina	22,834
Sargantay	Peru	22,542
Ojos del Salado	Argentine-Chile	22,539
Tupungato	Argentine-Chile	22,310
Huascarán	Peru	22,205

AMERICA (North)

McKinley	Alaska	20,320
Logan	Canada	19,850
Citlaltepao	Mexico	18,700
St Elias	Alaska	18,008
Popocatepetl	Mexico	17,887

OCEANIA

Sukarno	New Guinea	16,500

Some Volcanoes of the World

Volcano	Location	Height (in feet)
ACTIVE		
Antofalla	Argentina	20,103
Volcán Guayatiri (or Guallatiri)	Chile	19,882
Cotopaxi	Ecuador	19,612
Kluchevskaya	USSR	16,130
Mount Wrangel	USA	14,000
Mauna Loa	Hawaii	13,675
Cameroons	W. Cameroon	13,350
Mount Erebus	Ross Island, Antarctica	12,450
Nyiragongo	Zaire	11,560
Etna	Sicily	11,121
Chillan	Chile	10,500
Nyamuragira	Zaire	10,150
Villarica	Chile	9,325
Paricutin	Mexico	9,000
Asama	Japan	8,200
Ngauruhoe	New Zealand	7,515
Beeren Berg	Jan Mayen Island, Greenland Sea	7,470
Hecla	Iceland	5,100
Vesuvius	Italy	3,700
Stromboli	Lipari Island, Italy	3,000
BELIEVED EXTINCT		
Aconcagua	Chile – Argentina	22,976
Chimborazo	Ecuador	20,500
Kilimanjaro	Tanzania	19,340
Antisana	Ecuador	18,850
Elbruz	Caucasus	18,526
Popocatepetl	Mexico	17,540
Orizaba	Mexico	17,400
Karisimbi	Zaire	15,020
Mikeno	Zaire	14,780
Fujiyama	Japan	12,395

DORMANT

Volcan Llullaillaco	Chile – Argentina	22,058
Demavend	Iran	18,600
Pico de Teyde	Teneriffe	12,180
Semerou	Indonesia	12,050
Haleakala	Hawaii	10,032
Guntur	Indonesia	7,300
Tongariro	New Zealand	6,458
Tristan da Cunha	South Atlantic	6,000
Pelée	Martinique, W. Indies	4,430
Krakatoa	Sunda Strait, S. Pacific	2,600

The World's Biggest Deserts

Desert	Location	Approx. area (in sq. miles)
Sahara	Northern Africa	3,000,000 to 3,500,000
Libyan	Eastern part of the Sahara	650,000
Australian	Interior of Australia	600,000
Arabian	Arabian Peninsula, South-west Asia	500,000
Gobi	Central Asia, Mongolia	450,000
Patagonian	Argentina	260,000
Kalahari	Botswana	200,000
Great Sandy	North-western Australia	160,000
Great Victoria	South-west Central Australia	125,000
Syrian	Northern Saudi Arabia, South-eastern Syria, Western Iraq and North-eastern Jordan	125,000
Kara Kum	South Soviet Union	110,000
Nubian	North-eastern Sudan	100,000
Thar	North-western India and adjacent Pakistan	100,000

The World's Biggest Lakes

Name	Location	Area (sq. miles)
Caspian Sea*	Asia	170,000
Superior	North America	31,820
Victoria Nyanza	Africa	26,200
Aral Sea*	USSR	24,400
Huron	North America	23,010
Michigan	North America	22,400
Malawi	Africa	14,200
Tanganyika	Africa	12,700
Great Bear	Canada	11,660
Baikal	USSR	11,580
Great Slave	Canada	11,170
Erie	North America	9,940
Winnipeg	Canada	9,398
Maracaibo	South America	8,296
Ontario	North America	7,540
Balkhash	USSR	7,050
Ladoga	USSR	7,000
Chad	Africa	6,000
Nettiling	Baffin Land	5,000
Eyre	Australia	3,700

* Classified as lakes as they are completely landlocked.

The World's Most Famous Rivers

River	Outflow	Length (in miles)
Amazon	South Atlantic Ocean	4,195
Nile	Mediterranean	4,145
Mississippi-Missouri	Gulf of Mexico	3,710
Ob-Irtysh	Gulf of Ob	3,460
Yangtze	North Pacific	3,400
Zaire	Atlantic Ocean	3,000

Mekong	China Sea	2,800
Hwang-Ho (Yellow)	Yellow Sea (Pacific)	2,600
Niger	Gulf of Guinea	2,600
Volga	Caspian Sea	2,400
Mackenzie	Beaufort Sea	2,350
Yukon	Bering Sea	2,000
St Lawrence	Gulf of St Lawrence	1,800
Rio Grande	Gulf of Mexico	1,800
Orinoco	Atlantic Ocean	1,800
Danube	Black Sea	1,725
Indus	Arabian Sea	1,700
Euphrates	Persian Gulf	1,700
Brahmaputra	Bay of Bengal	1,680
Zambesi	Indian Ocean	1,633
Ganges	Bay of Bengal	1,560
Don	Sea of Azov	1,210
Rhine	North Sea	820
Seine	English Channel	482
Shannon	Limerick	240
Thames	North Sea	210

FOOTNOTE: When, in 1969, the National Geographic Society re-measured the length of the Amazon, they found it to be 4,195 miles. This figure dismisses the long-held claim of the Nile to be the world's longest river.

Great Ship Canals

Name	Country	Opened	Length (in miles)
Gota	Sweden	1832	115
Suez	Egypt	1869	100
Kiel	Germany	1895	61
Panama	USA	1914	50·5
Elbe and Trave	Germany	1900	41

Longest Bridges

Bridge	Location	Length (in feet of waterway)
Oosterschelde Road Bridge	Netherlands	16,476
Lower Zambesi	Africa	11,322
Storsstromsbroen	Denmark	10,499
Tay Railway Bridge	Scotland	10,289
Upper Sone	India	9,839

The longest chain-stay bridge in the world was opened in October 1975. It snakes across the River Loire for 3,670 yards, near St Nazaire.

Longest Railway Tunnels

Name	Country	Miles	Yards
Simplon	Switzerland–Italy	12	560
Apennine	Italy	11	880
St Gotthard	Switzerland	9	550
Lötschberg	Switzerland	9	130
Mont Cenis	Italy	8	870

(The London Underground *Northern Line* between East Finchley and Morden, by the City Branch, uses tunnels totalling 17 miles 528 yards in length.)

Distance of the Horizon

The limit of distance to which one can see varies with the height of the spectator.

At a height of:	The range is:
5 ft.	2·9 miles
50 ft.	9·3 miles
100 ft.	13·2 miles
1,000 ft.	41·6 miles
5,000 ft.	93·1 miles
20,000 ft.	186·2 miles

The Seven Wonders of the Ancient World

The Pyramids of Egypt
The Hanging Gardens of Babylon
The Statue of Zeus at Olympia
The Temple of Artemis at Ephesus
The Tomb of Mausolus at Halicarnassus
The Colossus of Rhodes
The Pharos of Alexandria

The Seven Wonders of the Middle Ages

The Colosseum, Rome
The Catacombs of Alexandria
The Great Wall of China
Stonehenge
The Leaning Tower of Pisa
The Porcelain Tower of Nankin
The Mosque of St Sophia at Constantinople

4 POPULATION

World Population

The estimated total population of the world in mid-1973 was 3,860 millions. Progressive mid-year estimates:

Date	Millions	Date	Millions
AD 1	c. 200–300	1969	3,538
1650	c. 500–550	1970	3,632
1750	750	1971	3,706
1850	1,240	1972	3,782
1950	2,486	1975	4,022
1965	3,289	1985	4,933
1967	3,420	2007	7,600

Approximately one-half of the world population is accounted for by the population of four countries – China (mainland), India, the Union of Soviet Socialist Republics and the United States of America.

The world population has doubled in the last 50 years. It is expected to double again in the next 35 years. It is now estimated that the world's population in the year 2000 will be more than 6,000 million and possibly closer to 7,000 million.

If the present 'population explosion' continues it is calculated that there will be one person to each square yard by AD 2600 and humanity would weigh more than the Earth itself by AD 3700.

It is estimated that during the three months from April to June, 1975, 41,500 people came to live in the United Kingdom and 47,000 left. Returns for births and deaths in 1975 show 602,126 births and 579,773 deaths, giving an increase of 22,353.

Total Population of the Continents (mid-1973)

	Estimated Population (in millions)
Europe	472
Asia	2,204
USSR	250
Africa	374
America	545
Oceania	20·6

Total Population of the United Kingdom (mid-1975 Provisional)*

The total estimated population of the United Kingdom in mid-1975 was 55,962,100.

England and Wales	49,218,700
Scotland	5,206,200
Northern Ireland	1,537,200

*Office of Population Censuses and Surveys

Ten Largest Cities in Britain (by Population) in mid-1975*

	Estimated Total
London	7,111,500
Birmingham	1,084,600
Glasgow	880,600
Leeds	749,000
Sheffield	559,800
Liverpool	548,800
Manchester	506,300
Edinburgh	470,100
Bradford	460,600
Bristol	420,100
Belfast	368,200

*Office of Population Censuses and Surveys

Countries of the World and their Population (latest Census)

	Population
Europe	
Albania	1,626,315
Andorra	5,664
Austria	7,456,403
Belgium	9,650,944
Bulgaria	8,227,866
Channel Islands	123,063
Czechoslovakia	14,344,986
Denmark	4,937,784
Faeroe Islands	37,122
Finland	4,598,336
France	49,778,540
Germany, Federal Republic of	60,650,599
German Democratic Republic	17,068,318
Gibraltar	26,833
Hungary	10,322,099
Iceland	204,930
Ireland	2,978,248
Isle of Man	56,289
Italy	53,770,331
Liechtenstein	21,350
Luxembourg	332,434
Malta	315,765
Monaco	23,035
Netherlands	11,461,964
Norway	3,888,305
Poland	32,642,270
Portugal	8,668,267
Rumania	19,103,163
Spain	34,040,658
Sweden	8,076,903
Switzerland	6,269,783
Yugoslavia	20,522,972

Asia

Bahrain	216,078
Bangladesh	50,853,721
Bhutan	1,034,774
Brunei	136,256
Burma	28,885,867
China	590,194,715
Cyprus	577,615
Hong Kong	3,948,179
India	547,949,809
Indonesia	118,309,059
Iran	25,785,210
Iraq	8,047,415
Israel	3,124,000
Japan	104,665,171
Jordan	1,706,226
Khmer Republic	5,728,771
Korea	25,120,174
Kuwait	737,909
Lebanon	2,126,325
Macau	248,636
Malaysia	10,319,324
Maldives	103,801
Mongolia	1,197,600
Nepal	11,555,983
Pakistan	64,892,000
Palestine	1,035,821
Philippines	36,684,486
Portuguese Timor	610,500
Sikkim	204,760
Singapore	2,074,507
Sri Lanka	12,711,143
Syrian Arab Republic	6,304,685
Thailand	34,397,374
Turkey	35,666,549
United Arab Emirates	179,126
Yemen, Democratic	1,590,275

USSR	241,720,134
Byelorussian SSR	9,002,338
Ukrainian SSR	47,126,517

Africa

Algeria	11,821,679
Angola	5,673,046
Botswana	608,656
Cape Verde Islands	272,071
Central African Republic	1,202,910
Chad	3,254,000
Dahomey	2,106,000
Egypt	30,075,858
Equatorial Guinea	245,989
Ghana	8,559,313
Guinea	2,570,219
Ivory Coast	3,100,000
Kenya	10,942,705
Lesotho	852,361
Liberia	1,016,443
Malawi	4,039,583
Mauritania	1,030,000
Morocco	15,379,259
Mozambique	8,233,834
Namibia	526,004
Niger	2,501,800
Nigeria	55,670,055
Réunion	416,525
Rwanda	3,735,585
São Tomé and Principe	73,811
Senegal	3,109,840
Seychelles	52,650
Sierra Leone	2,180,355
South Africa	21,448,169
Southern Rhodesia	4,846,930
Sudan	10,262,536
Swaziland	374,697
Tunisia	4,533,351
Uganda	9,548,847
United Republic of Tanzania	12,313,469

Upper Volta	4,846,930
Zaire	12,768,706
Zambia	4,056,995

America (North)

Antigua	70,000
Belize	119,934
Bermuda	52,330
Canada	21,568,310
Cuba	8,553,395
Dominica	70,300
Dominican Republic	4,006,405
Greenland	39,600
Grenada	94,500
Guatemala	5,211,929
Haiti	4,243,926
Jamaica	1,865,400
Martinique	320,030
Mexico	48,225,238
Montserrat	11,458
Netherlands Antilles	188,914
Panama	1,428,082
Canal Zone	44,198
Puerto Rico	2,712,033
St Lucia	99,806
St Vincent	89,100
Trinidad and Tobago	945,210
United States of America	203,235,298

America (South)

Argentina	23,362,204
Bolivia	2,704,165
Brazil	92,341,556
Colombia	17,484,508
Ecuador	4,649,648
French Guiana	44,392
Guyana	714,000
Paraguay	2,354,071
Peru	13,572,052
Surinam	324,211
Uruguay	2,595,510
Venezuela	10,721,522

Oceania

American Samoa	27,159
Australia	12,755,638
British Solomon Islands	160,998
Christmas Island	2,691
Cook Islands	618
Fiji	476,727
French Polynesia	119,168
Gilbert and Ellice Islands	53,517
New Hebrides	77,988
New Zealand	2,862,631
Pacific Islands	90,940
Tonga	77,429
Western Samoa	146,635

Main Languages of the World

Language	Speakers (in millions)	Language	Speakers (in millions)
Mandarin (China)	493	Italian	58
English	291	Urdu (Pakistan and India)	54
Russian	167		
Hindi	162	Cantonese (China)	45
Spanish	155	Javanese (Indonesia)	42
German	123	Ukrainian (mainly USSR)	41
Japanese	98		
Bengali (India, Pakistan)	85	Telegu (India)	41
		Wu (China)	39
Arabic	82	Tamil (India and Sri Lanka)	37
Portuguese	80		
French	73	Min (China)	36
Malay	71	Korean	35

Expectation of Life at Birth

China	1965–70	Both sexes:	50·0
Japan	1972	Male 70·49	Female 75·92
Austria	1972	Male 66·8	Female 74·1
Czechoslovakia	1970	Male 66·23	Female 72·94
Denmark	1970–71	Male 70·07	Female 75·9
UK (England and Wales)	1970–72	Male 68·9	Female 75·1
France	1971	Male 68·5	Female 76·1
Australia	1960–62	Male 67·92	Female 74·18
Greece	1960–62	Male 67·46	Female 70·7
USSR	1968–69	Male 65·0	Female 74·0
Hungary	1970	Male 66·28	Female 72·05
Italy	1964–67	Male 67·87	Female 73·36
Canada	1956–67	Male 68·75	Female 75·18
Spain	1960	Male 67·32	Female 71·90
United States	1972	Male 67·4	Female 75·2
Sweden	1972	Male 71·97	Female 77·41
Switzerland	1960–70	Male 69·21	Female 75·03

The Seven Ages of Man

'All the world's a stage,
And all the men and women merely players:
They have their exits and their entrances;
And one man in his time plays many parts,
His acts being seven ages'.

Shakespeare *As You Like It*,
Act II, Sc. vii.

Quadragenarian	=	40–49 years old
Quinquagenarian	=	50–59 years old
Sexagenarian	=	60–69 years old
Septuagenarian	=	70–79 years old
Octogenarian	=	80–89 years old
Nonagenarian	=	90–99 years old
Centenarian	=	aged 100 or more

The greatest authenticated age to which a human being has ever lived is 113 years 214 days. Mrs Delina Filkins (née Ecker) was born at Stark, Herkimer County, New York, on 4 May 1815 and died at Richfield Springs, New York on 4 December 1928.

Wedding Anniversaries

Wedding anniversaries are named from the custom of giving a distinctive anniversary gift. The three most important are known as the silver wedding (after 25 years), the golden (after 50 years), and the diamond (after 60, 70 or 75 years).

Not all anniversaries have symbolic names – but here are a few of the most usual ones:

1st cotton	7th woollen	30th pearl
2nd paper	8th bronze	35th coral
3rd leather	9th pottery	40th ruby
4th silk	10th tin	45th sapphire
5th wooden	15th crystal	50th gold
6th sweets	20th china	55th emerald
	25th silver	60th diamond

5 THE WONDERS OF NATURE

The Animal Kingdom

All living things are either animals or plants. The Animal Kingdom consists of mammals, birds, reptiles, amphibians, fishes, insects and other invertebrates. It includes man as well as tiny one-celled organisms – animals so small that sometimes even the experts have difficulty in distinguishing them.

The Animal Kingdom can be easily divided into two – animals with backbones (vertebrates) and those without (invertebrates). Birds, reptiles, amphibians, fishes and mammals make up the vertebrate animals. Mammals and birds, unlike the other vertebrates, are warm blooded. They maintain a constant temperature. A rise in the temperature of Man is usually a sign of illness. Fishes, amphibians and reptiles have no regular body temperature – it changes with the temperature of the surroundings.

All mammals, except for a few primitive ones which lay eggs, bear their young alive. Even the ones that lay eggs suckle their young.

If we trace back the history of the various classes of vertebrates we find that the fishes gave rise to the first amphibians, the amphibians to the first reptiles and so on. The changes took place gradually.

MAN SHARES THE EARTH with an estimated 3,000,000,000,000,000,000, 000,000,000,000,000 (3,000 quintillion or 3×10^{33}) other living things.

THE LARGEST LIVING ANIMAL known today in the world is the Blue or Sulphur Bottom Whale (*Balaenoptera musculus*), which grows to a maximum of 100 feet long.

THE LARGEST LIVING LAND ANIMAL is the African bush elephant (*Loxodonta africana africana*). The average adult bull weighs 5·7 tonnes and stands 3·20m at the shoulder.

THE SMALLEST? Of all free-living organisms the smallest is a pleuro-pneumonia-like organism of the *Mycoplasma*. One of these, *Mycoplasma Laidlawii*, has a diameter of 0·000004 of an inch in its early life. The strain of *Mycoplasma* known as H 39 weighs an estimated $1·0 \times 10^{-16}$ of a gramme. Thus a 174-ton blue whale would weigh 177,000 trillion times as much!

Collective Nouns

Ants	Colony	Locusts	Plague
Apes	Shrewdness	Magpies	Tidings
Badgers	Cete	Nightingales	Watch
Bass	Shoal	Owls	Parliament
Bears	Sloth	Partridges	Covey
Caterpillars	Army	Peacocks	Ostentation
Cats	Clowder	Pheasants	Covey
Cattle	Drove	Plovers	Congregation
Chickens	Peep	Ponies	String
Crows	Murder	Pups	Litter
Doves	Dule	Rabbits	Nest
Ducks	Balding	Ravens	Unkindness
(on water)	Paddling	Rhinoceroses	Crash
Eggs	Clutch	Rooks	Building
Fish	School	Seals	Pod
Foxes	Skulk	Sheep	Flock
Geese (on water)	Gaggle	Sparrows	Host
(in flight)	Skein	Squirrels	Dray
Hares	Husk	Starlings	Murmuration
Hawks	Cast	Storks	Mustering
Hens	Brood	Swallows	Flight
Herons	Siege	Toads	Knot
Horses	Harras	Trout	Hover
Jellyfish	Smack	Turkeys	Rafter
Kittens	Kindle	Turtledoves	Pitying
Lapwings	Deceit	Turtles	Bale
Larks	Exaltation	Whales	Gam
Leopards	Leap	Wolves	Route
Lions	Pride	Woodpeckers	Descent

Well-known Animals of the World

Antelopes	Africa, Southern Asia, India.
Bears	North and South America, Europe, Northern Asia.
Buffaloes	(Water) India, Sri Lanka, Indo-China, Egypt, Philippine Islands.
	(African or Cape) Southern and Central Africa.
Camels	(Bactrian) The two-humped camels are found from China to Turkestan.
	(Dromedary) The one-humped camels live in the desert regions of Arabia and Egypt.
Chimpanzees	The forests of tropical Africa.
Elephants	India, Africa.
Foxes	(Red) Northern Europe, Asia and North America.
	(Grey) United States.
	(Arctic) Alaska, Greenland, northern Eurasia.
Giraffes	The tallest animals in the world. Africa.
Gorillas	Gorillas are the largest of the apes. They live in the forested areas of Central Africa.
Hippopotamuses	The deep rivers of Africa.
Hyenas	(Striped) From India to North Africa.
	(Brown) Southern Africa.
	(Spotted) Central and Southern Africa.
Kangaroos	Australia and New Guinea.
Koalas	Bear-like marsupial mammals of Australia.
Lions	Africa, Asia. Mountain lions (often called Cougars or Pumas) live in North and South America.
Llamas	South America.
Musk-Oxen	North America and Greenland.
Orang-Utans	Forests and jungles of Borneo and Sumatra.
Pandas	China and Tibet.
Reindeer	The Arctic regions of Europe and Western Asia.
Rhinoceroses	(Black) Africa.
	(White) Africa.
	(Great One-horned) Northern Bengal, Assam and Nepal.
Skunk	(Spotted) From Central America to Central United States.
Tapirs	Central America, Northern South America, Burma, Thailand, Malaya and Sumatra.
Tigers	Asia – from India to Siberia and Java.
Wolves	Found in the cold regions throughout the Northern Hemisphere.
Zebras	Africa.

Periods of Gestation and Incubation

Species	Usual Period	Species	Usual Period
Ass	365–374 days	Guinea Pig	63–70 days
Bitch	63 days	Hen	21 days
Camel	45 weeks	Human	273 days
Canary	14 days	Mare	336 days
Cat	56 days	Mouse	18–19 days
Cow	280 days	Pigeon	18 days
Duck	28 days	Rabbit	32 days
Elephant	2 years	Rat	21–24 days
Ewe	147–150 days	Sow	112 days
Goat	151 days	Turkey	28 days
Goose	30 days	Zebra	56 weeks

Points of a Horse

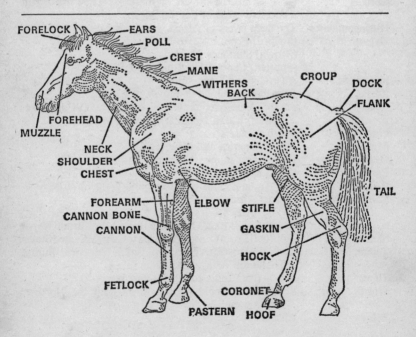

FORELOCK · EARS · POLL · CREST · MANE · WITHERS · BACK · CROUP · DOCK · FLANK · FOREHEAD · MUZZLE · NECK · SHOULDER · CHEST · FOREARM · CANNON BONE · CANNON · ELBOW · STIFLE · GASKIN · HOCK · TAIL · FETLOCK · CORONET · PASTERN · HOOF

Horse Talk

Colt	Male horse under the age of four.
Filly	Female horse under the age of four.
Foal	A colt or filly up to the age of 12 months.
Gelding	Castrated stallion.
Mare	The female.
Stallion	A horse capable of reproducing the species.

Life Cycles of Mammals

	Maximum recorded life (in years)		Maximum recorded life (in years)
Antelope	15	Horse	20
Badger	14	Kangaroo	17
Bear (Brown)	34	Lion	20–30
Camel	40	Monkey (Marmoset)	16
Cat	21	Mouse	2
Chimpanzee	25	Otter (European)	11
Cow	20	Pig	15
Dog	20	Porcupine	20
Elephant (Indian)	70	Rabbit	6
Ewe	12	Reindeer	15
Fox	12	Rhinoceros	40
Gerbil	5	Sea-lion	23
Giraffe	27	Shrew (Common)	$1\frac{1}{2}$
Guinea-pig	6	Squirrel	10
Hamster (Golden)	1–2	Tiger	20
Hedgehog	3	Whale	24
Hippopotamus	40		

Birds of the World

Birds form a very large branch of the Animal Kingdom. The sequence of Orders is as follows:

1. **Passeriformes (Perching Birds)** – Crow, Raven, Rook, Jackdaw, Magpie, Jay, Chough, Starling, Hawfinch, Greenfinch, Goldfinch, Siskin, Linnet, Bullfinch, Crossbill, Chaffinch, Brambling, Corn-Bunting, Yellow-Bunting (or Yellow-Hammer), Reed-Bunting, House Sparrow, Tree Sparrow, Skylark, Woodlark, Meadow-Pipit, Tree-Pipit, Pied Wagtail, Grey Wagtail, Yellow Wagtail, Nuthatch, Great Tit, Blue Tit, Coal Tit, Long-tailed Tit, Red-backed Shrike, Spotted Flycatcher, Goldcrest, Firecrest, Chiffchaff, Willow-Warbler, Reed-Warbler, Blackcap, Whitethroat, Missel-Thrush, Song Thrush, Blackbird, Redwing, Wheatear, Stonechat, Redstart, Nightingale, Robin, Hedge-Sparrow, Wren, House Martin, Sand-Martin.
2. **Apodiformes** – Swifts.
3. **Caprimulgiformes** – Nightjars.
4. **Coraciiformes** – Bee-eaters, Hoopoe, Kingfisher.
5. **Piciformes** – Woodpeckers, Wrynecks.
6. **Cuculiformes** – Cuckoos.
7. **Strigiformes** – Owls.
8. **Falconiformes (Birds of Prey)** – Peregrine Falcon, Merlin, Kestrel, Golden Eagle, Common Buzzard, Sparrow-Hawk, Goshawk, Kite, Osprey.
9. **Ciconiiformes** – Storks, Spoonbills, Ibises, Herons, Bitterns, Flamingoes.
10. **Anseriformes** – Swans, Geese, Ducks.
11. **Pelecaniformes** – Gannets, Cormorants.
12. **Procellariiformes** – Petrels.
13. **Podicipitiformes** – Grebes.
14. **Colymbiformes** – Divers.
15. **Columbiformes** – Pigeons, Doves.
16. **Charadriiformes** – Curlew, Whimbrel, Woodcock, Common Snipe, Dunlin, Sandpiper, British Redshank, Plover, Oyster-Catcher, Gulls, Terns, Skuas, Auks, Puffins.
17. **Gruiformes** – Bustards, Cranes, Rails, Moorhens, Coots.
18. **Galliformes (Game Birds)** – Grouse, Ptarmigan, Pheasant, Partridge, Quail.

Parts of a Bird

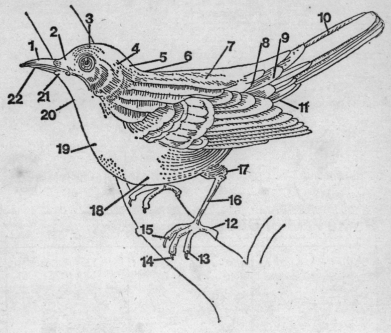

1. Upper Part (Bill)	12. Hind Toe
2. Forehead	13. Outer Toe
3. Crown	14. Middle Toe
4. Ear Coverts	15. Inner Toe
5. Nape	16. Tarsus (Elongated Ankle)
6. Neck	17. Tibia (Shin Bone)
7. Back	18. Belly
8. Rump	19. Breast
9. Upper Tail Coverts	20. Throat
10. Tail Feathers	21. Chin
11. Under Tail Coverts	22. Lower Part (Bill)

S—B

Some Bills of Birds

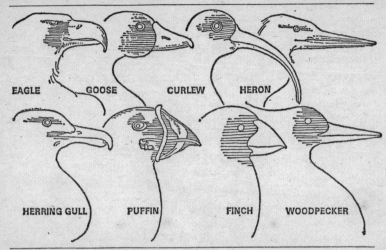

EAGLE   GOOSE   CURLEW   HERON

HERRING GULL   PUFFIN   FINCH   WOODPECKER

Some Feet of Birds

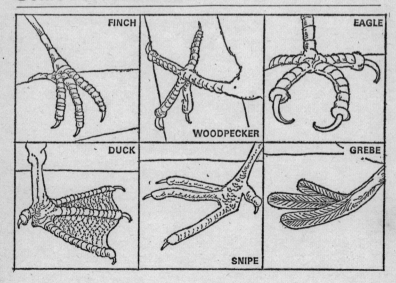

FINCH   EAGLE

WOODPECKER

DUCK   GREBE

SNIPE

Life Cycles of Birds

The average life expectancy of a bird in the wild is very short. These figures show the maximum recorded life-span for an individual of each species to the nearest year.

Blackbird	9	Black Headed Gull	30
Black Cap	5	Herring Gull	32
Bullfinch	8	Jackdaw	14
Chaffinch	10	Jay	18
Tree Creeper	4	Kestrel	16
Collared Dove	3	Magpie	15
Stock Dove	8	Mallard	20
Dunnock	8	House Martin	6
Fieldfare	5	Moorhen	11
Spotted Flycatcher	8	Nuthatch	9
Canada Goose	11	Barn Owl	15
Greenfinch	10	Little Owl	16
Wood Pigeon	14	Song Thrush	14
Rock-Pipit	5	Blue Tit	10
Redstart	7	Coal Tit	5
Redwing	19	Great Tit	10
Robin	11	Long-tailed Tit	4
Rook	20	Marsh Tit	10
Starling	20	Turnstone	20
House Sparrow	11	Grey Wagtail	3
Tree Sparrow	10	Pied Wagtail	6
Swallow	16	Great Spotted Woodpecker	9
Mute Swan	19	Green Woodpecker	5
Swift	21	Wren	5
Missel-Thrush	10	Yellow-Hammer	7

There are 8,600 known living species of birds. The flightless North African ostrich – *Struthio Camelus Camelus* – is the largest, reaching a height of 2·74 m and a weight of 156·5 kg. Helena's humming-bird – *Mellisuga helenae* – is the smallest bird in the world. An average adult male measures 58 mm and weighs about 2 g.

Freshwater Fishes

This list gives the names of some of the many freshwater fishes that inhabit the waters of the British Isles. The Families are as follows:

1. **Petromyzonidae** – the Lampreys.
2. **Acipenseridae** – the Sturgeon.
3. **Clupeidae** – the Shads.
4. **Salmonidae** – the Salmon, Trout, Char, Whitefish, Grayling.
5. **Osmeridae** – Smelt (or Sparling).
6. **Esocidae** – the Pike.
7. **Cyprinidae** – Carp, Barbel, Gudgeon, Tench, Minnow, Chub, Dace (or Dart), Roach, Rudd, the Breams, the Bleak.
8. **Cobitidae** – the Loaches.
9. **Anguillidae** – the Common Eel.
10. **Gadidae** – the Burbot.
11. **Serranidae** – the Bass or Sea Perch.
12. **Percidae** – the Perch, Pope (or Ruffe).
13. **Mugilidae** – the Mullets.
14. **Cottidae** – the Bullhead (or Miller's Thumb).
15. **Gasterosteidae** – the Sticklebacks.
16. **Pleuronectidae** – the Flounder.

Parts of a Fish

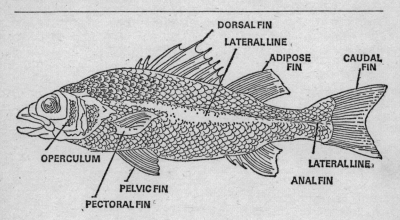

Life Cycles of Fishes

	Maximum length of life (in years)		Maximum length of life (in years)
Cod	13	Pike	15
Goldfish	10	Plaice	22
Haddock	14	Salmon	13
Herring	18	Sturgeon	25
Perch	10		

THE LARGEST FISH CAUGHT IN A BRITISH RIVER was a common sturgeon. It was caught in the Esk, Yorkshire, in 1810 and weighed 208 kg.

THE SHORTEST RECORDED FRESHWATER FISH and the smallest of all vertebrates is the dwarf pygmy goby, found in the lakes of Luzon in the Philippines. Adult males measure only 7·5 to 9·9 mm in length and weigh 4 to 5 mg.

Arthropoda

The Arthropoda is the largest division of the Animal Kingdom, forming about three-quarters of the known species. This is the class to which the Insects belong. Arthropoda comes from two Greek words meaning 'having jointed feet' but, in fact, it is the legs rather than the feet which are jointed.

The most important groups of Arthropoda are: Insecta, Arachnida, Crustacea, Diplopoda and Chilopoda.

1 – **Insecta.** It is estimated that about five out of every six animal species in the world are insects. There are about 20,000 named species in Britain alone and about 3 million species or more in the world – and more are being discovered each year. There are twenty-five Orders of British Insects. The best-known of the very small, primitive, wingless insects are the Silverfish and the Firebrat, which are common in buildings in the British Isles. Of the winged insects the following are the ones we see most:

Dragonfly
Mayfly

Cockroach
Stonefly
Earwig
Cricket
Grasshopper
Bugs (there are about 1,630 known species in Britain including Bedbug, Water Scorpion, Water Boatman, Froghoppers, Leaf-hoppers and Aphids – Greenfly and Blackfly)
Alder-fly
Snake-fly
Scorpion-fly
Caddis-fly (there are nearly 200 species of Caddis-fly. Fishermen use them as lures and some popular names for them are: the Great Red Sedge, Silverhorns and the Grannom)
Butterflies and Moths (c. 2,190 British species)
House Fly, Gnat, Mosquito (c. 5,200 British species)
Fleas
Ants, Bees, Wasps (over 6,000 British species)
Beetles and Weevils (c. 3,690 British species)

2. **Arachnida** – The majority of this group are land animals. They range in size from tiny mites no more than 0·1 mm long to the enormous black spider of Africa which is 180 mm long. They are chiefly predators, and live on other insects.

The best-known dwellers in our surroundings are:
*Spiders
Mites
Ticks
Tail-less Whip Scorpions
Whip Scorpions
Daddy Longlegs (or Harvestmen)
Sun Spiders (solpugids)

*There are 603 known British species of spider, covering an estimated population of more than 500,000,000,000,000. The most venomous spider in the world is probably the 'black widow' of the Americas. Females have a bite capable of killing a human being.

The world's largest known spider is the 'bird-eating' spider of northern South America. A male specimen, collected in French Guiana in 1925, had a body length of 8·9 cm and a leg span of 25 cm when fully extended.

The rarest in Britain is the black and crimson Eresus Niger which has been recorded less than a dozen times. The smallest spider found in Britain is the money spider (*Glyphesis cottonae*). Adults have a body length of 1 mm.

3. **Crustacea** – Crustacea are sometimes known as the 'insects of the sea'. There is scarcely a ditch or pond where some, at least, of the more minute forms cannot be found. On land they are less common. They play a part in the seas and oceans similar to that played by insects on land. There is a multitude of crustacea that do not have popular names. Among the most familiar are:
   Crabs
   Lobsters
   Woodlice
   Crayfish
   Prawns
   Shrimps
   Sandhoppers
   Barnacles
   Water fleas

4. **Diplopoda** – These are the Millipedes. They have two pairs of legs to each segment of the body, with the exception of the first three segments.

5. **Chilopoda** – or Centipedes. The word 'Centipede' means 'hundred-footed' but the number of legs varies from 15–173 pairs, depending on the species. Centipedes have only one pair of legs to a segment.

THE COMMONEST INSECTS are the Springtails (Order *Collembola*). Calculations showed that in one acre of grassland the top 228 mm of soil contained 230,000,000.

THE LARGEST of the 21,000 species of insect found in Britain is the rare death's-head hawk moth (*Acherontia atropos*). Females have a body length of 60 mm, a wing span of up to 133 mm and weigh about 1·6 g.

THE SMALLEST insects are 'Hairy-winged' beetles, and 'Battledore-wing fairy flies' (Parasite wasps). They are 0·2 mm long and the fairy flies have a wing span of 1 mm.

THE RAREST BUTTERFLY is the giant birdwing (*Troides allottei*) found in the Solomon Islands.

THE LONGEST LIVED insects are the Queen termites, which have been known to lay eggs for up to 50 years.

Parts of an Insect

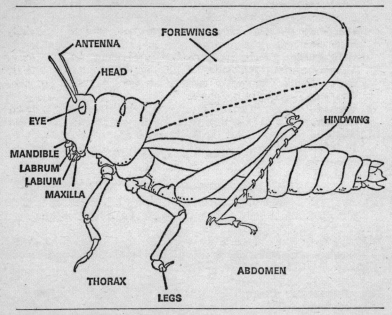

Some British Wild Flowers

This list gives the names of some British wild flowers, arranged in their botanical families:

1. **Buttercup Family** – Buttercup, Marsh Marigold, Wood Anemone, Lesser Celandine, Traveller's Joy, Water Crowfoot, Monkshood, Columbine, Adonis.
2. **Pink and Cranesbill Families** – Ragged Robin, Red Campion, Maiden Pink, Greater Stitchwort, Meadow Cranesbill, Hemlock Storksbill.
3. **Forget-me-not and Parsley Families** – Forget-me-not, Hound's Tongue, Bugloss, Sea Holly, Hemlock.
4. **Figwort Family** – Ivy-Leaved Toadflax, Eyebright, Germander Speedwell, Yellow Toadflax, Foxglove.
5. **Rose Family** – Dog Rose, Herb Bennet, Wild Strawberry, Bramble, Agrimony, Cinquefoil, Crab Apple, Meadowsweet.
6. **Mint Family** – Red Dead Nettle, Water Mint, Marjoram, Ground Ivy, Hedge Woundwort.

7. **Wallflower and Primrose Families** – Wild Wallflower, Jack-by-the-Hedge, Shepherd's Purse, Lady's Smock, Primrose, Cowslip, Yellow Loosestrife, Scarlet Pimpernel.
8. **Pea Family** – Kidney Vetch, Red Clover, Broom, Bird's Foot Trefoil, Furze, Sainfoin.
9. **Daisy Family** – Daisy, Hemp Agrimony, Fleabane, Ox-Eye Daisy, Yarrow, Coltsfoot, Chicory, Nipplewort, Ragwort, Cat's Ear, Carline Thistle, Groundsel, Tansy, Cornflower, Dandelion, Burdock, Goat's Beard, Bristly Ox-Tongue.
10. **Various Families** – Red Poppy, Wood Sorrel, Sweet Violet, Wild Heartsease, Flax, Rose-Bay, Willow-Herb, Milkwort, Ivy, Field Scabious, Teasel, Goose-Grass, Honeysuckle, Lesser Periwinkle, Harebell, Lamb's-Tongue Plantain, Sea Lavender, Thrift, Heather, Bluebell, Cuckoo-Pint, Vernal Grass.

Parts of a Flower

BUTTERCUP

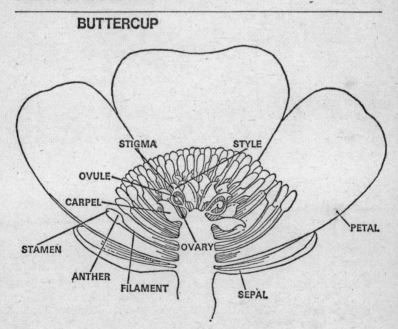

The Rarest Flowers in Britain

Specimens of many plants are only known in a single locality, so it is rather difficult to determine which is the rarest flower in Britain. But the following three may well qualify for the title:

The adder's-tongue spearwort
The flecked pink spurred coral-root (a British orchid)
The rose purple Alpine coltsfoot

Main Trees in Britain

The trees which grow in Great Britain are divided into two main groups: the *Angiosperms*, broad-leaved trees which can be deciduous or evergreen, and *Gymnosperms*, which comprise mainly coniferous trees and are, with few exceptions, evergreen.

Angiosperms

Alder	Lime (or Linden)
Almond	Magnolia
Apple	Maple
Ash	Mulberry
Aspen	Oak
Beech	Pear
Birch	Plane
Box	Plum
Buckthorn	Poplar
Cherry	Quince
Damson	Sloe
Elder	Sweet Bay (the true Laurel)
Elm	Sycamore
Hawthorn (or May)	Tamarisk
Hazel	Tulip Tree
Holly	Walnut
Hornbeam	White Beam
Horse Chestnut	Willow
Laburnum	Wistaria

Gymnosperms

Cedar

Common Spruce (Norway Spruce)

Cypress

Douglas Fir

Larch

Maidenhair Tree

Monkey Puzzle (or Chile Pine)

Scots Pine

Silver Fir

Yew

Tallest Trees in Great Britain (by Species)

	Location	*Height in metres*
Grand Fir	Leighton Park, Powys	56
Douglas Fir	Powis Castle, Powys	54
Spruce (Sitka)	Murthly, Tayside	53
Wellingtonia	Endsleigh, Devon	50
Hemlock (Western)	Benmore, Strathclyde	47
Silver Fir	Dupplin Castle, Tayside	46
Lime	Duncombe Park, North Yorks.	45
Plane	Bryanston, Dorset	44
Larch (European)	Bonskeid, Tayside	44
Pine (Corsican)	Stanage Park, Powys	43
Oak (Sessile)	Whitefield House, Hereford & Worcs	42
Eucalyptus (Blue Gum)	Glengarriff, County Cork	42

Some Trunks and Leaves

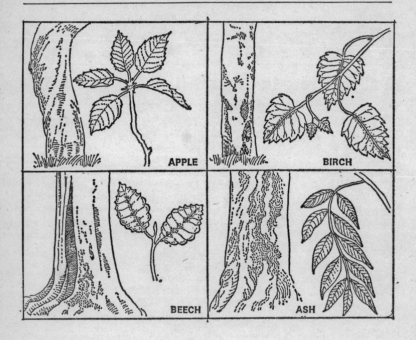

6 CODES

The Country Code

Damage done to the countryside every year, particularly at holiday seasons, is frightening. Most of it is unintentional; all the same, one thoughtless or careless action can ruin someone's livelihood. To keep visitors aware of this, and to guide their behaviour, the Countryside Commission prepared, in 1951, a Country Code, consisting of ten maxims based on common sense – and common failings. It runs like this:

1. Guard against all risk of fire.
2. Fasten all gates.
3. Keep dogs under proper control.
4. Keep to paths across farm land.
5. Avoid damaging fences, hedges and walls.
6. Leave no litter.
7. Safeguard water supplies.
8. Protect wild life, wild plants, and trees.
9. Go carefully on country roads.
10. Respect the life of the countryside.

The Dog Owners' Code

Do keep him well under control in the country, and always on the lead if there is livestock about. Even well-behaved dogs may chase and savage livestock unless restrained, and an animal savaged by a dog suffers pain and terror beyond description. (In one year, dogs killed 6,000 sheep and 20,000 poultry.)

Do exercise him regularly. He needs a good run, off the lead – but not where he can run on to a road, and not near livestock.

Do keep him clean – frequent brushing is the best way and gives you a chance to look for pests, cuts, sores or bad ears.

Do see that he has somewhere to sleep that is dry and out of draughts. If he has a kennel, it should be raised off the ground and protected against both heat and cold.

Do feed him regularly – one or two good meals every day at the same time. He needs fresh water too.

Do have your name and address marked on his collar so that he can be brought home if he strays.

Don't let him run loose on the road. Dogs let loose on the highway are a danger to themselves and a menace to road users. In one year alone, 75,000 dogs suffered in road accidents and 3,000 people were killed or injured in road accidents in which dogs were involved.

Don't keep him tied up or shut up by himself for long periods – it will make him cross and snappy and too excited to control when he is released. Never leave him in a car with all the windows closed.

Don't delay before obtaining skilled attention if he seems ill. Meanwhile keep him warm. See that he has a drink and something to eat if he wants it, but don't fuss him.

Don't let the children tease him when they are playing together.

Don't let him worry the neighbours by barking unchecked, and don't let him foul pavements or grass verges.

Don't keep a dog unless you are prepared to take the trouble to look after him properly and to train him in obedience.

A dog that is not healthy and well-trained is a misery to himself, an annoyance to neighbours, a danger to livestock and traffic and a nuisance to his owner. A healthy, well-trained dog is a contented dog, a trusty friend and guardian, and a companion who spreads happiness all round.

The Green Cross Code

1. **First find a safe place to cross, then stop.**
   It is safer to cross at some places than others. Subways. Footbridges. Zebra and Pelican crossings. Traffic lights. Where there is a policeman, or a lollipop man, or a traffic warden. If you can't find any good crossing places like these choose a place where you can see clearly along the roads in all directions. Don't try to cross between parked cars. Move to a clear space and always give drivers a chance to see you clearly.

WRONG   RIGHT

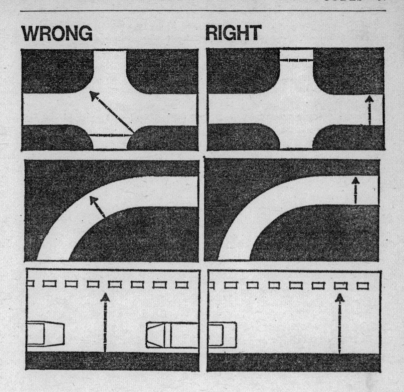

2. **Stand on the pavement near the kerb.**
   Don't stand too near the edge of the pavement. Stop a little way back from the kerb where you'll be away from traffic, but you can still see if anything is coming.

3. **Look all round for traffic and listen.**
   Traffic may be coming from all directions, so take care to look along every road. And listen too, because you can sometimes hear traffic before you can see it.

4. **If traffic is coming, let it pass. Look all round again.**
   If there's any traffic near let it go past. Then look round again and listen to make sure no other traffic is coming.

5. When there is no traffic, walk straight across the road.
When there is no traffic near it's safe to cross. If there is something in the distance do *not* cross unless you're certain there's plenty of time. Remember, even if traffic is a long way off it may be coming very fast. When it's safe, walk straight across the road – don't run.

6. Keep looking and listening for traffic while you cross.
Once you're in the road, keep looking and listening in case you didn't see some traffic or in case other traffic suddenly appears.

7 THE WEATHER

Clouds

The proper study of clouds began when an English chemist, Luke Howard, gave Latin names to a few obviously different cloud forms in 1803. The terms he gave to the three main forms, which became the basis of the internationally accepted cloud classification, are: *cumulus* (Latin for 'heap'); *cirrus* ('curl' or 'hair'); and *stratus* ('layer').

Meteorologists now divide clouds into ten types.

A. The HIGH CLOUDS (mean heights 16,500 to 45,000 – 5 to 13 km) are called '*Cirrus*', '*Cirrocumulus*' and '*Cirrostratus*'.

Cirrus clouds, which look rather like curly white wisps of hair drawn out in plumes across a blue sky, are also known as 'Mare's-tail' or 'paint-brush'. They are the highest clouds in the sky. The temperature where they lie is below freezing point and the particles are really clouds of ice crystals. Sailors believe *cirrus* in a blue sky foretells windy weather.

Cirrocumulus looks rather like the white caps on the ocean or the ripples in the sand on the sea-shore. These small cloud patches are often seen after a depression at the approach of fair weather.

The appearance in the sky of *Cirrostratus*, a transparent, whitish cloud veil, which does not obscure the sun or moon, usually means that rain is on the way. The refraction of the sun's rays by the ice crystals often causes a halo round the sun or moon.

B. The MIDDLE CLOUDS (mean heights 6,500 to 23,000 – 2 to 7 km) are known as '*Altocumulus*', '*Altostratus*' and '*Nimbostratus*'.

Altocumulus are large rounded white or greyish masses of clouds with shadows, often arranged in wavy lines, sometimes broken into 'popples' by the intersection of two sets of waves. The wave form is caused by the flow of one air-layer over another differing in temperature, density or humidity. In summer they can often be seen in the early morning or late evening.

Altostratus, a sure sign of rain, gives a thin, continuous grey or bluish cloud sheet through which the sun barely shines. This 'watery-sky' is caused by a current of warm moist air flowing up over a cold front.

Nimbostratus, dark grey and threatening clouds, are thick enough to blot out the sun. The base and edges are usually ragged and separate fragments ('scud') are torn from the base by strong winds.

C. The LOW CLOUDS (mean heights 0 to 6,500 – 0 to 2 km) are '*Stratocumulus*', '*Stratus*', '*Cumulus*' and '*Cumulonimbus*'.

The first of these, *Stratocumulus*, are large lumpy masses of dark grey or whitish cloud – a lower and heavier form of the Middle Cloud, *Altocumulus*.

Stratus, uniform layers of grey cloud with a fairly uniform base, often thickens and turns to fog, drizzle or rain. It is the lowest type of cloud, and when the sun is visible its outline is clearly seen through the cloud.

Cumulus are heavy, detached, dome or cauliflower-shaped clouds with sharp outlines and flat bases. The sunlit parts are brilliant white.

Cumulonimbus clouds tower up to a far greater height than the cumulus. They are the massive, lowering thunderclouds that can stretch through all cloud levels. Powerful ascending currents carry the cloud to heights where rain, snow and hail are formed.

The Colours of the Rainbow

Violet, Indigo, Blue, Green, Yellow, Orange, Red.

Coastal Weather Forecast Areas

The map opposite is Crown Copyright, reproduced with the permission of the Controller of Her Majesty's Stationery Office

This map shows the boundaries of the coastal sea areas referred to in the shipping forecasts.

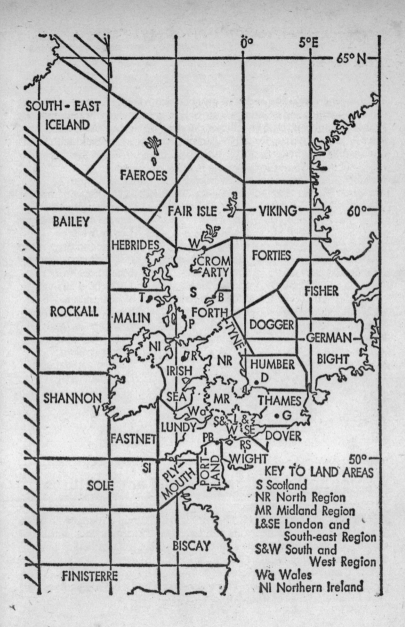

65° N

0° 5°E

SOUTH - EAST
ICELAND

FAEROES

FAIR ISLE VIKING 60°

BAILEY

HEBRIDES W

CROM
ARTY

FORTIES

S B FISHER

ROCKALL T

MALIN FORTH

P DOGGER

NI TYNE GERMAN

R NR BIGHT

IRISH HUMBER

SEA D

SHANNON MR THAMES

V Wa G

LUNDY S& L&

W SE DOVER

FASTNET PB RS

WIGHT 50°

SI WIGHT

SOLE PLY- PORT- KEY TO LAND AREAS
MOUTH LAND S Scotland
NR North Region
MR Midland Region
L&SE London and
South-east Region
S&W South and
West Region
BISCAY Wa Wales
NI Northern Ireland

FINISTERRE

The Beaufort Scale

The Beaufort Scale is a series of numbers from 0 to 17, to designate the force of the wind. The numbers 0 to 12 were arranged by Admiral Sir Francis Beaufort in 1806 to indicate the strength of the wind from a calm, force 0, to a hurricane, force 12 – 'that which no canvas could withstand'. The Beaufort numbers 13 to 17 were added by the US weather bureau in 1955.

Beaufort Number	Miles Per Hour	Description	Observation
0	0–1	Calm	Smoke rises vertically
1	1–3	Light Air	Smoke drifts slowly
2	4–7	Slight breeze	Leaves rustle
3	8–12	Gentle breeze	Leaves and twigs move
4	13–18	Moderate breeze	Small branches move
5	19–24	Fresh breeze	Small trees sway
6	25–31	Strong breeze	Large branches sway
7	32–38	Moderate gale	Whole trees move
8	39–46	Fresh gale	Twigs break off trees
9	47–54	Strong gale	Branches break
10	55–63	Whole gale	Trees snap and are blown down
11	64–75	Storm	Widespread damage
12	More than 75	Hurricane	Extreme damage
13	·83–92		
14	93–103		
15	104–114	Hurricane	
16	115–125		
17	126–136		

Fahrenheit and Centigrade Temperatures

Gabriel Daniel Fahrenheit (1688–1736) was a German physicist who made important improvements in the construction of thermometers and introduced the thermometric scale known by his name. It had a boiling point at 212° and a freezing point at 32°.

The Centigrade thermometer was invented by Anders Celsius (1701–1744), a Swedish astronomer. This Celsius scale had a boiling point at 100° and a freezing point at 0° (zero).

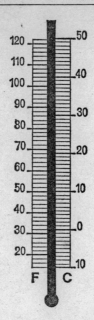

To convert Fahrenheit into Centigrade: subtract 32, multiply by 5 and divide by 9.
To convert Centigrade into Fahrenheit: multiply by 9, divide by 5 and add 32.

8 TIME

The Seasons of the Year

'Four seasons fill the measure of the year;
There are four seasons in the mind of man'.
(Sonnet *The Human Seasons*, Keats)

The year is divided into four seasons – Spring, Summer, Autumn and Winter – each associated with a stage of vegetation and a type of weather. The seasons are defined astronomically to begin about the 21st day of March, June, September and December.

Spring, the first season of the year, begins at the Vernal Equinox – the time at which the Sun crosses the Equator and day and night are of equal length all over the world.

Summer, the second and warmest season, begins at the Summer Solstice, the time at which the Sun is farthest from the Equator and seems to stay still before returning. Sunrise and sunset show no variation for several days. The longest day is June 21st or 22nd.

Autumn, the third season, begins astronomically at the Autumnal Equinox, when the Sun crosses from North to South of the Equator and causes night and day to be of equal length.

Winter, the fourth and coldest season of the year, begins at the Winter Solstice and ends at the Vernal Equinox. Midwinter is marked by the shortest day – usually December 22nd.

The Months

January   (Lat. *Ianuarius*) Although named for Janus, the two-faced
          Roman god of beginnings, January was the eleventh month,
          not the first, until about 153 BC.

February (Lat. *Februarius*) The twelfth month of the early Roman
          calendar primarily devoted to ceremonies of purification, in
          anticipation of the New Year, hence its name derived from
          the root of Februare, 'to purify'.

March   (Lat. *Martius*) Originally the first month and the beginning
          of the annual cycle of religious festivals. Named for the god
          Mars, the god of war.

April   (Lat. *Aprilis*) The month considered by the Romans sacred
          to Venus. Its name is thought to originate either from that of
          Aphrodite, her Greek equivalent, or from the Lat. *aperire*
          ('to open'), referring to the unfolding of buds and blossoms
          at this season.

May   (Lat. *Maius*) The origin is uncertain: some derive it from
          Maiores meaning 'elders'; others from Maia, a goddess,
          whose name meant 'increase'.

June   (Lat. *Iunius*) The name is possibly connected with that of the
          goddess, Juno, though some Roman authorities preferred
          to think that this month honoured the young and favoured
          the derivation 'iuniores' – the opposite of 'maiores' (see
          May).

July   (Lat. *Iulius*) The fifth month in the early Roman calendar,
          originally called Quintilis. It was renamed in honour of Julius
          Caesar in 44 BC, the year of his death.

August   (Lat. *Augustus*) The sixth month in the early Roman calendar,
          originally called Sextilis. It was renamed after the Emperor
          Augustus in 8 BC.

September (Lat. *Septem*) As is shown by its Latin name, it was the seventh
          month in the early Roman calendar. *Septem* means seven,
          and *imber* a shower of rain, from the rainy season usually
          beginning at this time of year.

October   (Lat. *Octo*) The eighth month in the early Roman calendar.
          Ghosts, hobgoblins and witches of Hallowe'en are relics of a
          pre-Christian Celtic feast of the dead held at this season.

November (Lat. *Novem* 'nine') The ninth month in the ancient Roman
          calendar, when the year began in March. The old Saxon
          name was *Wind-monath* (wind month) when the fishermen

drew their boats ashore and ceased fishing until the next
spring.

December (Lat. *Decem* 'ten') Some features survive in the traditional
observances connected with Christmas of both the Roman
Saturnalia which was celebrated in December and a great
mid-winter festival held by the ancient Teutonic peoples.

The Days of the Week

Sunday (Old English: *Sunnendaeg*) The first day of the week, anciently
dedicated to the Sun.

Monday The second day of the week: called by the Anglo-Saxons
Monandaeg, i.e., the day of the Moon.

Tuesday The third day of the week. Named after Tiu, son of Odin, and
a younger brother of Thor.

Wednesday The fourth day of the week, Woden's (or Odin's) Day.

Thursday The day of the god Thor. The French call it '*jeudi*', Jove's
day. Both Jove and Thor were gods of thunder and formerly
Thursday was sometimes called Thunderday.

Friday The sixth day of the week: in ancient Rome called *dies
Veneris*, the day dedicated to Venus, hence the French
vendredi. Northern nations adopted the same naming system
and the nearest equivalent to Venus was Frigg or Freyja,
hence Friday.

Saturday The seventh day of the week: called by the Anglo-Saxons
Saeterdaeg, after the Latin *Saturni dies*, the day of Saturn.

The Date Line

The Date Line, where each calendar day begins, is a zig-zag line that coin-
cides approximately with the 180th meridian. The date must be set back
one day when crossing in an easterly direction, and put forward one day
when crossing in a westerly direction.

It is indicated by joining up the following nine points:

Lat.	Long.	Lat.	Long.	Lat.	Long.
60°S.	180°	15°S.	172½°W.	53°N.	170°E.
51°S.	180°	5°S.	180°	65½°N.	169°W.
45°S.	172½°W.	48°N.	180°	75°N.	180°

World Time Chart

Area	Standard time (difference from GMT in hours)
Afghanistan	$+4\frac{1}{2}$
Albania	+1
Aleutian Islands	−11
Andaman Islands	$+6\frac{1}{2}$
Angola	+1
Antigua	−4
Argentina	−4
Australia	
(a) Victoria, New South Wales, Queensland, Tasmania	+10
(b) N. Territory, S. Australia	$+9\frac{1}{2}$
(c) West Australia	+8
Austria	+1
Azores	−2
Bahamas	−5
Bahrain	+3
Bangledesh	+6
Barbados	−4
Bermuda	−4
Bolivia	−4
Botswana	+2
Brazil	
(a) East including all coast and Brasilia	−3
(b) West	−4
(c) Territory of Acre	−5
British Honduras	−6
Brunei	+8
Bulgaria	+2
Burma	$+6\frac{1}{2}$
Canada	
(a) Newfoundland	$-3\frac{1}{2}$

Area	Standard time (difference from GMT in hours)
(b) Atlantic Zone: Labrador, New Brunswick, Nova Scotia, Prince Edward Is., Quebec (East of Pte. des Monts)	−4
(c) Eastern Zone: North-West Territory (East), Ottawa, Ontario, Quebec (West of Pte. des Monts)	−5
(d) Central Zone: Manitoba, North-West Territory (Central)	−6
(e) Mountain Zone: Alberta, North-west Territory (Mountain) Saskatchewan	−7
(f) Pacific Zone: British Columbia, North-west Territory (West)	−8
(g) Yukon Territory: White-horse and Watson Lake Dawson City and Mayo	−9
Cape Verde Islands	−2
Central African Republic	+1
Chile	−4
China	
(a) Chungking, Lanchow	+7
(b) Peking, Shanghai	+8
Christmas Island (Indian Ocean)	+7
Congo, Republic of	+1
Cook Islands	$-10\frac{1}{2}$
Costa Rica	−6
Cuba	−5
Cyprus	+2
Czechoslovakia	+1

Area	Standard time (difference from GMT in hours)	Area	Standard time (difference from GMT in hours)
Denmark	+1	Jamaica	−5
Dominica	−4	Japan	+9
Dominican Republic	−5	Jordan	+2
Ecuador	−5	Kenya	+3
Egypt	+2	Korea	
Ethiopia	+3	(a) North Korea	+9
Falkland Islands	−4	(b) Republic of Korea	
Fiji	+12	(South)	+9
Finland	+2	Kuwait	+3
French Guiana	−4	Laos	+7
Germany	+1	Latvia, USSR	+2
Greece	+2	Lebanon	+2
Greenland		Leeward Islands	−4
(a) Scoresby Sound	−2	Lesotho	+2
(b) Angmagssalik, West		Libya	+1
Coast except Thule	−3	Lithuania	+1
(c) Thule area	−4	Luxembourg	+1
Grenada	−4	Madeira	−1
Guinea	−1	Malawi	+2
Guyana	−3¾	Malaysia, Federation of	
Haiti	−5	(a) West Malaysia	
Honduras	−6	(Malaya)	+7½
Hong Kong	+8	(b) East Malaysia (Sabah,	
Hungary	+1	Sarawak)	+8
India	+5½	Maldive Islands	+5
Indonesia		Malta	+1
(a) Western Zone: Java,		Mauritania	−1
Sumatra, Bali, Madura	+7	Mauritius	+4
(b) Central Zone: Borneo,		Mexico	
Celebes, Timor	+8	(a) Mexico City	−7
(c) Eastern Zone: Molucca		(b) Baja California Sur,	
Islands, Kai, Aroe, West		States of Sonora, Sinaloa	
Irian	+9	and Nayarit	−7
Iran	+3½	(c) Baja California Norte	−7
Iraq	+3	Mozambique	+2
Ireland	+1	Nepal	+5½
Israel	+2	New Guinea	+10
Italy	+1	New Zealand	+12

Area	Standard time (difference from GMT in hours)	Area	Standard time (difference from GMT in hours)
Nicaragua	$-5\frac{3}{4}$	Uganda	$+3$
Nigeria	$+1$	United Kingdom	$+1$
Norway	$+1$	United States of America	
Pakistan	$+5$	(a) Eastern Zone	-5
Panama	-5	(b) Central Zone	-6
Papua	$+10$	(c) Mountain Zone	-7
Paraguay	-4	(d) Pacific Zone	-8
Peru	-5	(e) Alaska:	
Philippine Islands	$+8$	Ketchikan to Skagway	-8
Poland	$+1$	(f) Hawaiian Islands	-10
Puerto Rico	-4	Uruguay	$-3\frac{1}{2}$
Rhodesia	$+2$	USSR	
Salvador	-6	(a) Kiev, Leningrad,	
Santa Cruz Islands	$+11$	Moscow, Odessa	$+3$
Saudi Arabia	$+3$	(b) Archangel, Volgograd	$+4$
Senegal	-1	(c) Omsk	$+6$
Seychelles	$+4$	(d) Vladivostok	$+10$
Singapore	$+7\frac{1}{2}$	Venezuela	$-4\frac{1}{2}$
Solomon Islands	$+11$	Vietnam	
Somalia	$+3$	(a) North Vietnam	$+7$
South Africa, Republic of	$+2$	(b) Republic of Vietnam	
Sri Lanka	$+5\frac{1}{2}$	(South)	$+8$
Sudan	$+2$	Virgin Islands	-4
Sweden	$+1$	Windward Islands	-4
Switzerland	$+1$	Yemen	$+3$
Syria	$+2$	Yugoslavia	$+1$
Tahiti	-10	Zambia	$+2$
Taiwan	$+8$	Zaire	
Tanzania (Tanganyika and Zanzibar)	$+3$	(a) Kinshasa	$+1$
		(b) Kivu, Katanga, Kasai	$+2$
Thailand	$+7$		
Tonga (Friendly Islands)	$+13$		
Trinidad and Tobago	-4		
Tunisia	$+1$		
Turkey	$+2$		

9 COMMUNICATIONS

The Post Office

There are 23,390 Post Offices in the UK (including 21,804 sub Post Offices). For the year ending 31 March 1976 the Post Office handled 30,349 million first class and 62,429 million second class inland letters. 6,252 million overseas letters were handled, 5·8 million overseas parcels and 158·2 million inland parcels.

Postage stamps were sold to the value of £326·3 million, Inland Money Orders issued to the value of £9·3 million, Overseas Money Orders issued to the value of £16 million. The total number of Postal Orders issued was 224·8 million to the value of £502.7 million.

LETTER POST SINCE 1897:

After	June 22nd, 1897	4 oz for 1d
	Nov. 1st, 1915	1 oz for 1d; 2 oz for 2d; 4 oz for 2½d
	June 3rd, 1918	4 oz for 1½d; 6 oz for 2d
	June 1st, 1920	3 oz for 2d
	May 29th, 1922	1 oz for 1½d; 3 oz for 2d
	May 14th, 1923	2 oz for 1½d
	May 1st, 1940	2 oz for 2½d
	Oct. 1st, 1957	1 oz for 3d; 2 oz for 4½d
	May 17th, 1965	2 oz for 4d; 4 oz for 6d
	Sept. 16th, 1968	Two-Tier Letter Service introduced

INLAND POSTAL RATES FROM 7 JUNE 1976:
LETTER POST   PARCEL POST

Not Over	First Class	Second Class	Not Over	Ordinary Parcels	Local Parcels
60 g (2·1 oz)	8½p	6½p	1 kg (2·2 lb)	55p	45p
100 g (3·5 oz)	11½p	9p	2 kg (4·4 lb)	70p	60p
150 g (5·3 oz)	15p	11p	3 kg (6·6 lb)	85p	75p
200 g (7·1 oz)	18½p	14p	4 kg (8·8 lb)	100p	90p
250 g (8·8 oz)	22p	17p	5 kg (11·0 lb)	110p	99p
300 g (10·6 oz)	25½p	20p	6 kg (13·2 lb)	120p	109p
350 g (12·3 oz)	29p	23p	7 kg (15·4 lb)	130p	119p
400 g (14·1 oz)	32½p	26p	8 kg (17·6 lb)	140p	129p
450 g (15·9 oz)	36p	29p	9 kg (19·8 lb)	150p	139p
500 g (1·1 lb)	39½p	32p	10 kg (22·0 lb)	160p	149p
750 g (1·7 lb)	57p	47p max.			

Each extra 250g*
(8·8 oz)*   17½p
* or part thereof

AIR MAIL EUROPE

Air Mail labels are not necessary.
Letters and Postcards are sent by air whenever this will result in earlier delivery.

LETTERS

Not Over	20 g	50 g	100 g	250 g	500 g	1 kg	2 kg
	10p	18p	24p	48p	92p	106p	260p

POSTCARDS   7p

Talking With Deaf People

1. Face them directly.
4. Don't shout – speak slowly and distinctly.
2. Try to give a visual indication of what you are saying.
3. Use short sentences – each with a single thought.

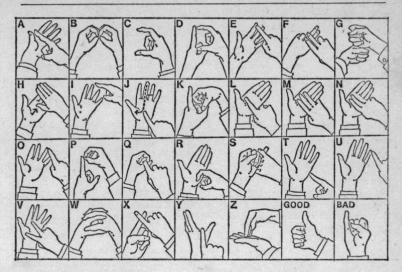

Finger Spelling Alphabet
(Reproduced by courtesy of the British Deaf Association).

International Morse Code

The Morse Code was invented by Samuel Morse in 1838 as a means of sending messages by telegraph. The following are the rules for spacing:

1. A long is equal to three shorts.
2. The space between elements which form the letter, figure or symbol is equal to one short.
3. The space between 2 letters, figures, or symbols is equal to three shorts (i.e. one long).
4. The space between two words is equal to five shorts.

Letter	Character	Letter	Character	Letter	Character	Letter	Character
A	· —	D	— · ·	G	— — ·	1	· — — — —
B	— · · ·	E	·	H	· · · ·	2	· · — — —
C	— · — ·	F	· · — ·	I	· ·	3	· · · — —

J	.---	P	.--.	V	...-	4	....-
K	-.-	Q	--.-	W	.--	5	.....
L	.-..	R	.-.	X	-..-	6	-....
M	--	S	...	Y	-.--	7	--...
N	-.	T	-	Z	--..	8	---..
O	---	U	..-			9	----.
						10	-----

Preliminary Call	-.-.-	Oblique Stroke	-..-.
Full Stop	.-.-.-	Brackets	-.--.-
Comma	--..--	Underline	..--.-
Apostrophe	.----.	Long Break Sign	-...-
Hyphen	-....-	Error	....
Inverted Commas	.-..-.	End of Message	.-.-.
Question	..--..	Finish of Transmission for an indefinite period	...-.-

Distress Signals

1. The best-known emergency signal is S O S, which some people take to mean 'Save Our Souls', made in Morse by radio or any available means. The Morse Code for S O S is ...---...
2. A signal sent by radio of the word 'mayday', from the French *m'aidez*, 'help me'.
3. A gun or other explosive signal fired at intervals of a minute.
4. A continuous sounding of any fog-signal apparatus.
5. A signal consisting of a square flag having above or below it a ball, or anything resembling a ball.

Wavebands Allocated to Broadcasting in the United Kingdom

Band	Frequencies*	Remarks
Long-wave (lf)	160–255 kHz (1,875–1,176 m.)	One frequency (200 kHz) assigned to BBC and used at Droitwich for Radio 2.

Medium-wave (mf)	525–1,605 kHz (571–187 m.)	Frequencies assigned to BBC for Radios 1, 2, 3 and 4 and local radio, including two international common frequencies, 1,484 kHz and 1,594 kHz. Two exclusive frequencies for BBC External Services to Europe. Frequencies for IBA local radio are also provided in this band.
Short-wave (hf)	3,950–4,000 kHz (75–m. band) 5,950–6,200 kHz (49–m. band) 7,100–7,300 kHz (41–m. band) 9,500–9,775 kHz (31–m. band) 11,700–11,975 kHz (25–m. band) 15,100–15,450 kHz (19–m. band) 17,700–17,900 kHz (16–m. band) 21,450–21,750 kHz (13–m. band) 25,600–26,100 kHz (11–m. band)	Frequencies in these bands are used as required by the BBC's External Services for broadcasting to Europe and overseas. The order of frequency for particular service areas depends upon diurnal and seasonal conditions.
Band I (vhf)	41–68 MHz	Five channels each 5 MHz wide for BBC 405-line television.
Band II (vhf)	87·5–100 MHz	Frequencies at present restricted to the sub-band 88–97·6 MHz and used for fm sound broadcasting Radios 2, 3 and 4 and local radio and IBA local radio.
Band III (vhf)	174–216 MHz	Eight channels each 5 MHz wide for BBC and IBA 405-line television.
Band IV (uhf)	470–582 MHz	Fourteen channels each 8 MHz wide for BBC and IBA 625-line television.

Band V (uhf)	614–854 MHz	Thirty channels each 8 MHz wide for BBC and IBA 625-line television.
Band VI (shf)	11,700–12,500 MHz	Allocated for both terrestrial and satellite broadcasting and likely to be the first band used for the latter service.
Band VII (ehf)	41–43 GHz	Allocated for satellite broadcasting.
Band VIII (ehf)	84–86 GHz	Allocated for satellite broadcasting.

* The relationship between frequency and wavelength is as follows:

$$\text{Wavelength (in metres)} = \frac{300}{\text{Frequency (in MHz)}}$$

Thus the wavelength corresponding to a frequency of 60 MHz is

$$\frac{300}{60} = 5 \text{ metres}$$

The frequency corresponding to a wavelength of 1,500 metres is

$$\frac{300}{1,500} = 0.2 \text{ MHz}$$

or 200 kHz (1 MHz = 1,000 kHz).

Greenwich Time Signal

THE TIME SIGNALS which are broadcast all over the world throughout the day are received by land line from the Royal Observatory Time Station at Herstmonceux in Sussex. On January 1st, 1972, the familiar six short pips were replaced by, normally, five short pips followed by a long one. The correct time is indicated, to an accuracy of $\frac{1}{20}$ of a second, by the beginning of the last pip.

Some Long-running Sound Radio Programmes

The longest-running sound radio programme is *The Week's Good Cause* which began on January 24th, 1926 and is still on the air.

The longest-running record programme? Roy Plomley's *Desert Island Discs* which began on January 29th, 1942.

The longest-running solo radio feature is Alistair Cooke's *Letter from America*, which was first commissioned as a series of talks on March 6th, 1946.

The longest-running radio serial is *The Archers*, which first went on the air on June 7th, 1950.

Some Long-Running Television Programmes

The longest-running television series on BBC is *Panorama*, the first transmission of which was on November 11th, 1953. *Andy Pandy* was first transmitted on June 11th, 1950, and *Come Dancing* on November 12th, 1951. The *News* has been featured since March 23rd, 1938.

The longest broadcast by the BBC was the coverage of the Coronation of Queen Elizabeth II on June 2nd, 1953. It lasted 7 hours 15 minutes – from 10.15 am to 5.30 pm.

On October 30th, 1973, Jonathan Dimbleby made an Appeal for victims of the Ethiopian and African Drought. It was broadcast on BBC-TV and IBA (Thames TV) and raised £1,520,000 – the largest amount raised by any TV appeal.

Some Important Dates in the Story of British Broadcasting

1922
14 Nov Daily broadcasting began from the London station of the British Broadcasting Company (2LO).

1923
28 Sep First issue of the *Radio Times* published.
30 Dec First Continental programme by landline from Radiola, Paris.
31 Dec First broadcast of chimes of Big Ben to usher in the New Year.

1924
 4 Apr Broadcasts for schools began.
23 Apr First broadcast speech by King George V from the opening of the British Empire Exhibition, Wembley.

1926
31 Dec The British Broadcasting Company dissolved.

1927
 1 Jan The British Broadcasting Corporation constituted under Royal Charter for ten years.

1929
16 Jan First issue of *The Listener* published.
21 Oct Brookmans Park station brought into service marking the beginning of the regional scheme.

1932
 2 May Broadcasting House, London, brought into service.
22 Aug First experimental television programme from Broadcasting House, 30-line system (Baird process taken over by BBC).
25 Dec First Round-the-Empire Christmas Day programme and broadcast message by King George V.

1936
 2 Nov High-definition Television Service from Alexandra Palace officially inaugurated.
11 Dec Abdication broadcast by HRH Prince Edward.

1937
12 May King George VI Coronation: first TV Service outside broadcast.

1938
 3 Jan First foreign-language service began (in Arabic).

1939
24 May First time Derby televised (scenes from course televised in 1938).
 1 Sep Television Service closed down for reasons of national defence.
 1 Sep Home Service replaced National and Regional Services.
 3 Sep Broadcasts by King George VI and the Prime Minister, Mr Neville Chamberlain, on the outbreak of war.

1940
 7 Jan Forces Programme began.

1944
27 Feb General Forces Programme began, replacing Forces Programme.

1945

29 Jul Light Programme introduced and Regional Home Services restarted.

1946

7 Jun Television Service resumed.

29 Sept Third Programme introduced.

1947

1 Jan General Overseas Service began.

1948

11 Oct First television outside broadcast from No 10 Downing Street: Commonwealth Conference.

1950

27 Aug First television outside broadcast from the Continent (Calais).

30 Sep First 'live' air to ground television broadcast (from an aircraft in flight).

1952

21 Apr First direct television from Paris (experimental).

5 May First schools television programme (4 weeks experiment).

1953

2 Jun Coronation ceremony televised for the first time.

15 Jun First television relay from ship at sea during the Royal Naval Review.

1954

6 Jun⎫
4 Jul⎭ First European exchange of television programmes with eight countries taking part.

1955

2 May First vhf radio broadcasting station brought into service at Wrotham.

20 Sep First issue of *TV Times* published.

22 Sep First ITV programmes transmitted in the London area.

1956

16 Jun First 'live' television broadcast from a submarine at sea.

4 Aug First television transmission from a helicopter.

5 Nov The first series of experimental colour television transmissions to include 'live' pictures from Alexandra Palace studios and Crystal Palace transmitter began.

1957
24 Sep BBC Television for schools began.
25 Dec Her Majesty the Queen's Christmas broadcast televised for the first time (heard simultaneously on radio).

1958
28 Oct State Opening of Parliament televised for the first time.

1959
17 Jun First public demonstration of transmission of films for television by transatlantic cable; first programme use June 18th, 1959.

1960
26 Mar Grand National televised for the first time.

1961
15 Feb Eclipse of the sun televised for BBC viewers from France, Italy, and Yugoslavia through Eurovision.
14 Apr First live television broadcast from Russia of welcome in Moscow of first 'space man', Major Gagarin.

 1 May Moscow May Day Parades seen 'live'.
10 Jun The first live television broadcast from London to USSR – Trooping the Colour.
 8 Jul First television broadcast from London to Hungary – Wimbledon tennis.

1962
20 Feb Transmission of first message from space from US astronaut Colonel John Glenn.
11 Jul First exchange of 'live' transatlantic programmes by satellite Telstar.
16 Jul First transmission of colour television by Telstar.

1964
 Mar First pirate radio station, Radio Caroline, began transmissions.
16 Apr First 'live' television relay from Japan to Europe via Telstar.
20 Apr First BBC-2 programmes on 625-lines transmitted from Crystal Palace.

1966
21 Apr Television cameras allowed in the House of Commons for the first time.

1967

1 Jul   BBC-2 began regular colour television transmissions using PAL system on 625-lines (first in Europe).

15 Aug   Ban on pirate radio broadcasting came into force in Great Britain.

30 Sep   Radio 1 introduced on 247 m. Radio networks renamed Radio 1, 2, 3, and 4.

8 Nov   BBC local radio experiment began from Leicester.

1968

6 Feb   First 'live' colour TV coverage of Olympic Games.

1969

16 May   Postmaster General announced start of colour television on ITV and BBC-1.

21 Jul   Man's first landing on the moon televised.

15 Nov   Colour television extended to BBC-1 and ITV on 625-lines vhf.

1970

2 Jul   State Opening of Parliament televised in colour for the first time.

1971

9 Jan   First issue of *Look In*, Junior *TV Times*, published.

10 Jan   Open University transmissions started on radio and BBC-TV.

16 Jun   Lord Reith died.

1972

20 Jan   Restrictions lifted on radio and television broadcasting hours.

14 Nov   50th anniversary of the first programmes broadcast by the British Broadcasting Company.

1973

24 Nov   BBC Radio Carlisle opened, completing the first 20 BBC local radio stations.

1974

10 Apr   Announcement of a Committee on the Future of Broadcasting under Lord Annan, followed by extension of the Royal Charter to 1979.

23 Sep   Regular CEEFAX service started.

1975

9 Jun–
4 July   Four-week parliamentary broadcasting experiment: live and recorded programmes from the House of Commons.

BBC LOCAL RADIO

There are 20 BBC local radio stations around Britain reaching more than 70% of the population:

Radio Birmingham	vhf 95·6	206m	Radio Manchester	vhf 95·1	206m
Radio Bristol	vhf 95·4	194m	Radio Newcastle	vhf 95·4	206m
Radio Humberside	vhf 95·3	202m	Radio Sheffield	vhf 88·6 & 95·05	290m
Radio London	vhf 95·3	206m	Radio Brighton	vhf 95·8	202m
Radio Merseyside	vhf 95·85	202m	Radio Carlisle	vhf 95·6	397m & 206m
Radio Oxford	vhf 95·0	202m	Radio Leicester	vhf 95·2	188m
Radio Stoke-on-Trent	vhf 94·6	200m	Radio Medway	vhf 97·0	290m
Radio Blackburn	vhf 96·4	351m	Radio Nottingham	vhf 94·8	195m
Radio Derby	vhf 96·5 & 94·2	260m	Radio Solent	vhf 96·1	301m & 188m
Radio Leeds	vhf 94·6	271m	Radio Cleveland	vhf 96·6	194m

The Independent Broadcasting Authority

On July 12th, 1972, the Independent Television Authority was re-named the Independent Broadcasting Authority and had its functions extended to cover the provision of Independent Local Radio.

The Independent Broadcasting Authority builds, owns and operates the transmitting stations which radiate ITV and ILR programmes, allocating transmitters to carry programmes originated by the various programme contractors.

The original VHF network was started with the opening of ITV programmes in the London area on September 22nd, 1955. The first batch of four of the new UHF transmitters, radiating the duplicated 625-line combined colour/black-and-white pictures in the PAL colour system, came into programme service on November 15th, 1969. The UHF network will continue to build up for many years.

The Independent Broadcasting Authority does not itself produce programmes.

Fifteen programme companies are under contract with the Authority to provide the programme service in fourteen areas for the six-year contract period until the end of July 1974, with an extension to 1979.

The programme companies obtain their revenue from the sale of advertising time in their own areas. Television advertisers can have nothing to do with programme production. They buy time in Independent Television just as they buy space in newspapers. They do not 'sponsor' programmes. The IBA controls the amount and distribution of advertising. The amount of advertising is limited to six minutes an hour, averaged over the day's programmes, with a maximum, normally, of seven minutes in any one clock hour. There is an average of three advertising intervals an hour.

Under the provisions of the Television Act, 1964, as amended by the Independent Broadcasting Authority Act, 1973, no programme sponsorship or advertising magazines will be permitted. Advertising time is to be sold for spot advertisements. These must be distinguishable as such and recognizably separate from one another and from the programme.

On radio, the maximum time allowed by the Authority for advertising in any hour is nine minutes.

From the outset of Independent Local Radio, the provision of a reliable news service was one of the most important elements in the programming. The first London commercial radio station to go on the air was the London Broadcasting Company which started on October 8th, 1973. Capital Radio, which broadcasts general entertainment programmes, started on October 16th, 1973.

INDEPENDENT LOCAL RADIO —
THE PROGRAMME COMPANIES

There are 19 Independent Local Radio stations in Great Britain.

In the 31 months between the first company going on air in October 1973 and the opening of Beacon Radio in Wolverhampton in April 1976 the Authority has, on average, brought a company on to air every six weeks.

In this time the total number of people in England, Scotland, Wales and Northern Ireland able to receive ILR has reached over 25 million on VHF and probably over 30 million on medium wave at some times of day.

ILR Belfast (Downtown Radio)	vhf 96·0 MHz	293m
ILR Birmingham (BRMB Radio)	vhf 94·8 MHz	261m
ILR Bradford (Pennine Radio)	vhf 96·0 MHz	235m
ILR Edinburgh (Radio Forth Ltd)	vhf 96·8 MHz	194m
ILR Glasgow (Radio Clyde Ltd)	vhf 95·1 MHz	261m
ILR Ipswich (Radio Orwell Ltd)	vhf 97·1 MHz	257m
ILR Liverpool (Radio City – Sound of Merseyside – Ltd)	vhf 96·7 MHz	194m
ILR London (Capital Radio Ltd)	vhf 95·8 MHz	194m
ILR London (London Broadcasting Co Ltd)	vhf 97·3 MHz	261m

ILR Manchester (Piccadilly Radio Ltd)	vhf 97·0 MHz	261m
ILR Nottingham (Radio Trent)	vhf 96·2 MHz	301m
ILR Plymouth (Plymouth Sound Ltd)	vhf 96·0 MHz	261m
ILR Portsmouth (Radio Victory)	vhf 95·0 MHz	257m
ILR Reading (Thames Valley Broadcasting)	vhf 97·0 MHz	210m
ILR Sheffield & Rotherham (Radio Hallam Ltd)	vhf 95·2 MHz (Sheffield)	194m
	vhf 95·9 MHz (Rotherham)	194m
ILR Swansea (Swansea Sound Ltd)	vhf 95·1 MHz	257m
ILR Teesside (Radio Tees)	vhf 95·0 MHz	257m
ILR Tyne/Wear (Metro Radio)	vhf 97·0 MHz	261m
ILR Wolverhampton/Black Country (Beacon Radio)	vhf 97·2 MHz	303m

The IBA Companies

Transmission Areas	Number of ITV/BBC Homes (000s)*
London	4,390
Midlands	3,050
Lancashire	2,570
Yorkshire	2,040
Central Scotland	1,265
Wales and the West	1,420
South	1,600
North East	925
East of England	1,180
South West	536
Ulster	404
Border	191
NE Scotland	347
All ITV areas	18,660**

*Jictar – estimate as at June, 1976.

**This figure does not equate with an addition of the individual area figures. This is because a percentage of homes are able to receive transmissions from more than one ITV area.

10 TRAVEL

A. Ships and the Sea

STRENGTH OF THE FLEET 1976/77

All HM Ships at Serials 1 to 10 and three of the Coastal Minesweepers/Minehunters at Serial 11 are assigned to NATO. The remaining ships would be retained under national control for tasks in support of NATO.

Type/Class	Operational, preparing for service or engaged in trials and training	Reserve or undergoing long refit, conversion, etc
Aircraft Carrier	1 ARK ROYAL	
ASW Carriers/Commando Ships	1 HERMES	1 BULWARK
Submarines	23	9
Polaris Submarines	REPULSE, RENOWN, REVENGE	RESOLUTION
Fleet Submarines	DREADNOUGHT, VALIANT, WARSPITE, CHURCHILL, SWIFTSURE, SOVEREIGN, SUPERB*	CONQUEROR, COURAGEOUS
OBERON Class	ORPHEUS, OBERSON, OTTER, ORACLE, OTUS, OCELOT, OSIRIS, OPOSSUM, OPPORTUNE	ODIN, OLYMPUS, ONSLAUGHT, ONYX
PORPOISE Class	NARWHAL, CACHALOT, WALRUS, FINWHALE	PORPOISE, SEA LION
Assault Ships	1 FEARLESS†	1 INTREPID
Cruisers	1 TIGER	1 BLAKE
Guided-Missile Destroyers	9	1
County Class	DEVONSHIRE, LONDON, FIFE, GLAMORGAN, NORFOLK, ANTRIM, KENT	
Type 82		BRISTOL
Type 42	SHEFFIELD, BIRMINGHAM*	

Type/Class	Operational, preparing for service or engaged in trials and training	Reserve or undergoing long refit, conversion, etc
General Purpose Frigates LEANDER Class	33 LEANDER, AJAX, GALATEA, AURORA, NAIAD, EURYALUS, PENELOPE†, ANDROMEDA, CHARYBDIS, HERMIONE, JUPITER, SCYLLA, BACCHANTE, ACHILLES, DIOMEDE, APOLLO, ARIADNE, CLEOPATRA, JUNO, DANAE	6 ARETHUSA, DIDO, PHOEBE, SIRIUS, MINERVA, ARGONAUT
Type 21	AMAZON, ANTELOPE, AMBUSCADE, ARROW*, ACTIVE*	
TRIBAL Class	ASHANTI, GURKHA, MOHAWK, NUBIAN, ESKIMO, TARTAR, ZULU	
MERMAID Class	MERMAID	
Anti-Aircraft Frigates Type 41		2 JAGUAR, LYNX
Aircraft Directional Frigates Type 61	2 SALISBURY, LLANDAFF	2 LINCOLN, CHICHESTER
Anti-Submarine Frigates	13 ROTHESAY, PLYMOUTH, RHYL, YARMOUTH, LOWESTOFT, FALMOUTH, BERWICK, BRIGHTON, EASTBOURNE†, TORQUAY†	2 LONDONDERRY
Type 14	KEPPEL, EXMOUTH, DUNDAS	HARDY
Mine Countermeasures	37	3
Coastal Minesweepers/ Hunters	BRONINGTON, BILDESTON, MAXTON, GAVINGTON, SHERATON, HUBBERTON, IVESTON, BOSSINGTON, KIRKLISTON, WILTON, NURTON, SHOULTON†, KELLINGTON, KEDLESTON, BRINTON, BRERETON, LEWISTON, GLASSERTON†, SOBERTON, WALKERTON, SHAVINGTON, CUXTON, FITTLETON, BICKINGTON, CRICHTON, CROFTON, HODGESTON, LALESTON†, ALFRISTON†, REPTON, WISTON, WOTTON†	UPTON, STUBBINGTON, POLLINGTON
Inshore Minesweepers	FLINTHAM†, DITTISHAM†, AVELEY†, THORNHAM†, ISIS†	
Fleet Maintenance Ship		1 TRIUMPH
Submarine Depot Ship	1 FORTH	
MCM Support Ship	1 ABDIEL	
Diving Trials Ship	1 RECLAIM	
Trials Ship	1 MATAPAN†	

Type/Class	Operational, preparing for service or engaged in trials and training	Reserve or undergoing long refit, conversion, etc
Coastal Patrol Vessels	5 YARNTON, MONKTON, WOLVERTON, WASPERTON, BEACHAMPTON	
Fast Target Boats	3 SABRE, SCIMITAR, CUTLASS	
Fast Patrol Boat/Patro Craft	4 CYGNET*, PETEREL*, TENACITY, KINGFISHER	
Seaward Defence Boats	2 DROXFORD†, DEE†	
Royal Yacht/Hospital Ship	1 BRITANNIA	
Ice Patrol Ship	1 ENDURANCE	
Survey Ships/Vessels	13 HECLA, HECATE, HYDRA, HERALD, BULLDOG, BEAGLE, FOX, FAWN, ECHO, EGERIA, ENTERPRISE, WOODLARK, WATERWITCH	
Submarine Tender	1 WAKEFUL	
Offshore Patrol Vessels	4 JURA‡, REWARD, JERSEY*, GUERNSEY*	
Patrol Craft	2 ALERT, VIGILANT	

Notes:

1. As this table includes ships due for completion or disposal during the course of the year, the sum of the numbers of each type is not an accurate indication of the number available at any one time.
2. Ships marked * will be under construction on March 31st, 1976 and are planned to enter Service during the year.
3. Ships marked † are engaged wholly or partially on trials and training.
4. ‡JURA will be returned to Department of Agriculture and Fisheries, Scotland later this year.
5. HM Ships approved for disposal during 1975/76: HAMPSHIRE, LEOPARD, HIGHBURTON, ARLINGHAM, BERRYHEAD.

NAVAL AIRCRAFT STRENGTH 1976/77

Aircraft type	Role	Deployment	No. of sqdns or flights	Notes
FIXED WING AIRCRAFT				
Buccaneer 2	Strike	Aircraft Carrier	1 Sqdn	NATO assigned
Gannet 3	AEW	Aircraft Carrier	1 Sqdn	NATO assigned
Gannet 3	AEW	RAF Lossiemouth	1 Sqdn	NATO earmarked
Phantom FG1	FGA	Aircraft Carrier	1 Sqdn	NATO assigned
HELICOPTERS				
Sea King	ASW	Aircraft Carrier	1 Sqdn	NATO assigned
Sea King	ASW	ASW Carrier	1 Sqdn	NATO assigned
Sea King	ASW	Cruiser	1 Sqdn	NATO assigned
Sea King	ASW	Prestwick	1 Sqdn	NATO assigned
Sea King	Aircrew training	RNAS Culdrose	1 Sqdn	NATO earmarked
Wasp	ASW	LEANDER Class Frigate	} 40 Flights	NATO assigned
Wasp	ASW	ROTHESAY Class Frigate		
Wasp	ASW	TRIBAL Class Frigate		
Wasp	ASW	Type 21 Class Frigate		
Wasp	ASW	Type 42 Destroyer		
Wasp	Aircrew training	RNAS Portland	1 Sqdn	NATO earmarked
Wessex 3	ASW	COUNTY Class Destroyers	7 Flights	NATO assigned
Wessex 3	Aircrew training	RNAS Portland	1 Sqdn	NATO assigned/ earmarked
Wessex 5	Commando assault	RNAS Yeovilton/ HERMES	2 Sqdns	NATO assigned
Wessex 5	Aircrew training	RNAS Yeovilton	1 Sqdn	NATO earmarked
Wessex 5	Fleet requirements	RNAS Portland	1 Sqdn	NATO earmarked

Abbreviations:

AEW	Airborne Early Warning.
FGA	Fighter/Ground Attack.
ASW	Anti-Submarine Warfare.
RNAS	Royal Naval Air Station.

Naval Ranks and Ratings

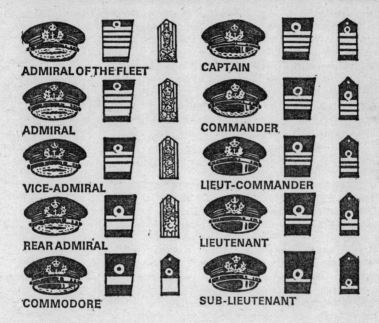

ADMIRAL OF THE FLEET

ADMIRAL

VICE-ADMIRAL

REAR ADMIRAL

COMMODORE

CAPTAIN

COMMANDER

LIEUT-COMMANDER

LIEUTENANT

SUB-LIEUTENANT

In addition to the above there are Midshipmen, Cadets, Warrant Officers, Chief Petty Officers and Petty Officers (the non-commissioned officers), leading seamen, able seamen and ordinary seamen.

The highest rank of Engineer Officers, Surgeon Officers and Accountant Officers or Paymasters, is that of Vice-Admiral, otherwise ranks are the same as those in the executive branch.

Sea Terms

ABAFT – Nearer the stern than (an object), e.g. abaft the gangway.
ADRIFT – Broken from moorings. Driven at random by tide and wind.
AVAST – To hold fast.
AWASH – Level with the surface of the water.

BELAY – To secure a rope to a cleat, belaying pin, or bollards.

BILGE – That part of a ship near the keel.

BROACH TO – Coming suddenly up to the wind.

BY THE HEAD – When a vessel is deeper in the water forward than aft she is said to be 'by the head'.

BY THE STERN – Opposite of 'by the head'.

CARRY AWAY – To break a spar or rope.

CHECK – To ease a rope a little. To stop progress.

CLAP ON – An order to get hold of a rope or purchase for the purpose of hauling on it.

DEAD WATER – The water in a vessel's wake close to her stern.

DRAG – A ship is said to be dragging when her anchor is not holding.

DRAUGHT – The depth of the lowest point of a ship or boat below the waterline.

EBB – The return of the tide-water towards the sea.

FLOW – The rise of the tide.

FREEBOARD – The height of a ship's upper deck above the waterline.

HAND OVER HAND – Hauling a rope quickly with alternate hands.

HANDSOMELY – Slowly and with care.

JACOB'S LADDER – A ladder made of rope or wire with wooden bars for steps.

LAND FALL – The first sight of land when at sea.

NEAP TIDES – Tides which rise least and fall least from the mean level.

SHEER – The rise of a ship's deck at the head and stern above the midship portion.

SHIPSHAPE – In proper seamanlike manner.

SMACK IT ABOUT – Get a move on.

STEERAGE WAY – When a vessel is moving with sufficient way to be steered.

TRIM – The condition of a ship with reference to how she floats on the water.

UNDER WAY – When a vessel is not at anchor or made fast to the shore or aground.

WEATHER TIDE – A tide that carries a vessel to windward.

WIND'S EYE – That point from which the wind blows.

YAW – When a ship does not steer a straight and steady course and her head moves from one side to the other, she is said to yaw about.

Parts of a Ship

STEM – The extreme front or foremost part of the ship.
STERN – The extreme rear or aftermost part of the ship.
BOW – That part of the ship's side which is near the stem.
QUARTER – That part of the ship's side which is near the stern.
BEAM – That part of the ship's side which lies between the bow and quarter.
STARBOARD SIDE – The right-hand side of a ship looking forward.
PORT SIDE – The left-hand side of a ship looking forward.
FORE AND AFT LINE – The line between the stem and stern – i.e. in line with the keel.
ATHWARTSHIPS – At right angles to the fore and aft line.
MIDSHIPS – Lying midway between stem and stern in a fore and aft line or midway between starboard and port in a thwartship line.
FORECASTLE (Also fo'c's'le) – The fore part of the upper deck.
QUARTERDECK – The after part of the upper deck.
WAIST – The midship part of the upper deck between the forecastle and quarter deck.
POOP – A short deck above the upper deck right aft in the stern.
TOPGALLANT FORECASTLE – A short deck above the upper deck, right forward over the forecastle.

Ship's Time

8 AM to Noon	Forenoon Watch
Noon to 4 PM	Afternoon Watch
4 PM to 6 PM	Dog Watches
6 PM to 8 PM	
8 PM to Midnight	First Watch
Midnight to 4 AM	Middle Watch
4 AM to 8 AM	Morning Watch

These times are kept by a bell being struck every half-hour, beginning with one at the first half-hour of the watch and ending with eight at the fourth hour of the watch except during the Dog Watches. During the Dog Watches, which are shorter in order to prevent the same watch having the same hours each day for duty, one bell is struck at 6.30 PM, two bells at 7 PM, three bells at 7.30 PM and eight bells at 8 PM.

Bends and Hitches

1. Bowline
2. Carrick Bend
3. Clove Hitch
4. Double Sheet Bend
5. Figure of Eight Knot
6. Fisherman's Bend
7. Reef Knot
8. Rolling Hitch
9. Running Bowline
10. Sheepshank
11. Single Sheet Bend
12. Timber Hitch

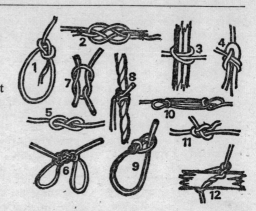

Sea Measures

1 Fathom = 6 feet

1 Cable = One-tenth of a nautical or sea mile, and measures 608 feet, or roughly 200 yards

1 Nautical or Sea Mile = 6,080 feet, or roughly 2,000 yards

1 Knot = Speed of 1 nautical or sea mile per hour

The Compass

The Magnetic Compass used for determining direction is operated by the magnetism of the earth.

A compass card is graduated in degrees clockwise from 000 (North) to 359, the circle being divided into 360 degrees. Directions are described as 'zero-four-five' (written 045°), 'three-two-eight' (328°) etc.

Magnetic compasses used to be graduated in points, each circle had 32 points, and each point represented 11¼ degrees. Some of these points are still used when referring to general directions:

The 4 Cardinal Points	N., E., S., and W.
The 4 Half-Cardinal Points	N.E., S.E., S.W., and N.W.
The 8 Intermediate Points	N.N.E., E.N.E.,
	E.S.E., S.S.E.,
	S.S.W., W.S.W.,
	W.N.W., N.N.W.

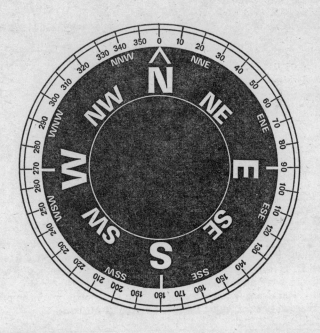

How to Find South in Daytime by Means of Your Watch

Hold your watch flat in your hand with the hour hand pointing to the sun. A line drawn halfway between the hour hand and the figure 12 on your watch will point to the South.

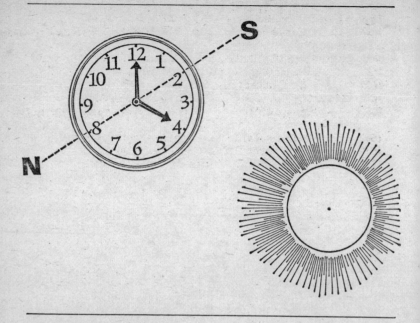

The Cinque Ports

The Cinque Ports were originally five in number: Dover, New Romney, Sandwich, Hastings and Hythe. After the Norman Conquest Rye and Winchelsea were added. Other members, known as 'limbs' are – Deal, Margate, Ramsgate, Tenterden, Faversham and Folkestone. The present Lord Warden of the Cinque Ports is Sir Robert Menzies.

Some Important Dates in the Story of the Sea

c. 1280 Mariner's Compass in general use.
1492–3 Columbus' first voyage of exploration; Bahamas discovered.
1495–6 First dry dock constructed at Portsmouth.
1498 Vasco da Gama reaches India by sea.

1508	First Marine Insurance in England.
1546	Henry VIII institutes the Navy Board for the maintenance of the Fleet.
1577	Drake sailed from Plymouth on his voyage round the world.
1591	The last fight of the *Revenge* (Aug. 31st).
1600	East India Company granted Charter.
1620	The *Mayflower* sails. Foundation of New England.
1637	Building of the *Sovereign of the Seas*, the first ship to carry 100 guns.
1660	The title General at Sea superseded by that of Admiral.
1675	Greenwich Observatory founded (Aug. 10th).
1740	Anson made his voyage round the world.
1748	Uniform for Officers adopted.
1757	Captain Campbell's Sextant supersedes the Quadrant.
1765	Launch of HMS *Victory*.
1768	Captain Cook's voyage to the Pacific in the *Endeavour*.
1776	Cook's voyage to find a navigable passage from the Pacific to the Atlantic over Canada. (He was killed in 1779.)
1789	Mutiny on the *Bounty*.
1794	Nelson loses the sight of his right eye at Calvi (July 10th).
1797	Mutiny at the Nore.
	Nelson loses his right arm at Santa Cruz (July 24th).
1798	Battle of the Nile (Aug. 1st).
1799	HMS *Lutine* wrecked.
1805	Battle of Trafalgar (Oct. 21st).
1806	Nelson buried in St Paul's (Jan. 9th).
1812	First steamboat, the *Comet*, plied on the Clyde.
1815	First steam vessel on the Thames.
1817	Present Custom House opened in London.
1818	First steamer crossed the Atlantic.
1822	Caledonian Canal opened.
1824	National Lifeboat Institution founded.
1825	First steam voyage to India.
1837	Shells, as substitute for Round Shot, made permissive in the British Navy.
1838	First regular Steamboat Service across Atlantic – voyage took 17 days.
	Screw propeller first used.
	The *Fighting Temeraire* is towed to her last berth.
1840	P & O Steam Navigation Company established.
1843	Gentlemen Volunteers rechristened Naval Cadets.
1848	North-West Passage discovered.

1851	First Submarine Telegraph.
1854	Napoleon III constructs 'Ironclads'.
1857	International Code of Signals established.
	Uniform for men adopted.
1858	*Great Eastern* steamer launched (Jan. 31st).
	First message by Atlantic Cable.
1860	First British sea-going steam ironclad battleship, *Warrior*, launched.
1861	Storm warnings first issued.
1863	Twin screws used.
1866	Atlantic cable laid by *Great Eastern*.
1867	The wooden three-decker *Victoria* was the flagship at the Review at Spithead, the last occasion on which a wooden ship of the line performed this office at a Review.
	Navigating Lieutenants substituted for Masters.
1869	Suez Canal opened (Nov. 17th).
1873	Royal Naval College, Greenwich, opened.
1881	Breech-loading principle accepted by Admiralty for big guns.
1887	Quick-firing principle applied to heavy guns.
1894	Manchester Ship Canal opened.
1895	Kiel Canal opened.
1900	Wireless Telegraphy adopted by Admiralty.
1901	New International Code of Signals in use. First wireless signals sent across Atlantic. First British submarine launched.
1904	First transatlantic turbine steamer *Victorian* launched.
1905	Wireless Telegraphy messages to ships at sea accepted by Post Offices.
1906	Launch of HMS *Dreadnought*.
1907	First British battle cruiser launched.
1912	Loss of *Titanic* – largest steamship afloat – and 1,513 lives.
1915	White Star Liner *Lusitania* sunk by German submarine.
1916	Battle of Jutland – last great fleet action for gunners.
1917	Unrestricted German U-Boat warfare commenced.
1918	Naval Mutiny at Wilhelmshaven. Surrender of the German High Seas Fleet.
1919	German Fleet scuttled at Scapa Flow.
1931	The Invergordon Mutiny.
1933	Italian liner *Rex* won the Blue Riband of the Atlantic – Gibraltar to Ambrose Lightship: 3,181 m. in 4 days, 13 hours, 58 minutes. Average speed: 28·92 knots.
1934	Mersey tunnel opened. Cunard White Star liner *Queen Mary* launched at Clydebank.

1935 French liner *Normandie* gained Blue Riband of the Atlantic. Southampton to Ambrose Light Vessel: 4 days, 11 hours, 33 minutes. Average speed: 29·68 knots.

1936 *Queen Mary* won Blue Riband of the Atlantic. Bishop Rock to Ambrose Light Vessel: 2,907 m. in 4 days, and 27 minutes. Average speed: 30·14 knots.

1938 *Queen Mary*: Bishop Rock to Ambrose Light Vessel in 3 days, 21 hours, 48 minutes. Average speed: 30·99 knots.

1941 Attack by the Japanese on the US Fleet at Pearl Harbor resulting in the entry into the war of Japan and USA.

1945 Surrender of the German Fleet. 156 U-Boats surrendered and 221 scuttled themselves.

1946 *Queen Elizabeth* left Southampton for New York on maiden voyage as passenger liner.

1947 *Queen Mary* left Southampton for New York on her first post-war passenger voyage.

1958 US nuclear submarine *Nautilus* made first passage under North Pole. She went beneath the pack ice off Point Barrow, Alaska, on August 1st, was at the North Pole on the 4th, and emerged from pack ice on the Greenwich meridian at 70°N on August 5th.
US nuclear submarine *Seawolf* remained submerged for 60 days during which she logged 13,700 miles.

1959 St Lawrence Seaway officially opened by Queen Elizabeth and President Eisenhower.

1961 Launch of nuclear submarine *Dreadnought*.

1963 Loss of US atomic submarine *Thresher* with 129 lives.

1966 Sir Francis Chichester left Plymouth on August 27th on the start of his single-handed, round-the-world voyage in *Gipsy Moth IV*. He arrived back in Plymouth Sound on May 28th, 1967.
Britain's first Polaris submarine, HMS *Resolution*, launched at Barrow by Queen Elizabeth, the Queen Mother. She carries 16 Polaris missiles as well as conventional torpedoes. (Went into service October 3rd, 1967.)

1967 British nuclear submarine HMS *Valiant* completed her submerged homeward journey from Singapore to the Clyde; a distance of 12,000 miles in 27 days, mostly at a depth below 200 ft.
Caning for juniors in the Royal Navy abolished. Wreck of Sir Cloudesley Shovel's flagship *Association*, sunk in 1707, found off the Isles of Scilly.
Queen Elizabeth II launched.
Queen Mary completed her last passenger voyage (later sold to US interests).

1968   Alec Rose completed his single-handed round-the-world voyage in his yacht *Lively Lady*.

Last passenger voyage of *Queen Elizabeth I* ended on Nov. 15th (sold to US then Hong Kong interests).

First Polaris missile to be fired from a British nuclear submarine launched from the *Resolution*.

1970   Prototype naval uniforms in radical new styles designed and tried out. Last issue of rum to the Royal Navy.

1971   HMS *Sheffield*, the Royal Navy's first Type 42 guided missile destroyer (its first warship to have all gas turbine propulsion) launched by HM the Queen at Barrow.

1972   *Queen Elizabeth I* capsized and sank in Hong Kong harbour.

Launching of HMS *Wilton*, a 153-ft. minehunter and the Royal Navy's first plastic warship.

1973   Keel of HMS *Invincible*, the first of the Royal Navy's anti-submarine cruisers, laid down at the Barrow Yard of Vickers Shipbuilding Group. The maritime Harrier and V/STOL aircraft is being developed for use in these ships.

HMS *Birmingham*, the second of the Sheffield class (Type 42) destroyers, launched.

1974   HMS *Hermes*, HMS *Devonshire*, HMS *Andromeda* and HMS *Rhyl*, and 41 Commando Royal Marines took part in evacuation of 21,000 people during Cyprus emergency.

Royal Navy Fleet Clearance Diving Team started work on clearance of unexploded ordnance in Suez Canal in conjunction with the Egyptian Armed Forces and the United States and French Navies.

1975   Keel of HMS *Broadsword*, the first of the Royal Navy's Type 22 frigates, was laid down at the shipyard of Yarrows (Shipbuilders) Ltd, Scotstown, Glasgow.

The first of the type 42 class destroyers, HMS *Sheffield*, enters service with the Royal Navy.

The Suez Canal is officially reopened (June).

1976   HMS *Jersey*, the first of the off-shore patrol ships launched.

HMS *Glasgow*, the 6th Sheffield class (Type 42) destroyer launched from the shipyard of Swan Hunters Shipbuilders, Newcastle-upon-Tyne.

HMS *London*, HMS *Bacchante* and HMS *Lowestoft* took part in the International Naval Review in the Hudson River, New York, part of the United States Bicentennial celebrations.

1977   Bell-bottom trousers, the black 'silk' kerchief, lanyard and tapes, which have been officially recognized as part of the 'square rig' uniform for junior ratings for more than a hundred years, abandoned in favour of a more modern dress.

B. Motor Cars and Roads

THE TOTAL MILEAGE of public roads in Great Britain (provisional figure as at April 1975) was 206,807, of which 156,636 were in England; 29,990 in Scotland; and 20,181 in Wales.

There were 20,538 miles of principal roads, 8,330 miles of trunk roads and 176,732 miles of other roads. Trunk and principal road motorways amounted to 1,207 miles.

Distance from London to Major Cities by Road

	Miles		Miles
Aberdeen	492	Exeter	170
Birmingham	110	Glasgow	392
Bristol	116	Gloucester	105
Cardiff	153	Holyhead	259
Dover	72	Inverness	531
Edinburgh	373	Leeds	190
Liverpool	197	Plymouth	211
Manchester	184	Sheffield	159
Newcastle upon Tyne	273	Southampton	77
Penzance	281	York	197

Registrations of New Vehicles

The Society of Motor Manufacturers and Traders list the number of registrations of new vehicles in the United Kingdom during the year ended December 1975 as a total of 797,338 British cars (368,671 of which were made by British Leyland) and a total of 396,750 imported cars (of which 64,010 were made by Datsun and 56,665 by Renault).

Index Marks – Vehicle Registration Numbers

A	London	AC	Warwickshire	AF	Cornwall
AA	Hampshire	AD	Gloucestershire	AG	Ayrshire
AB	Worcestershire	AE	Bristol	AH	Norfolk

AI	Meath	BT	Yorkshire	DF	Gloucestershire
AJ	Yorkshire	BU	Oldham	DG	Gloucestershire
AK	Bradford	BV	Blackburn	DH	Walsall
AL	Nottinghamshire	BW	Oxfordshire	DI	Roscommon
AM	Wiltshire	BX	Carmarthenshire	DJ	St Helens
AN	London	BY	London	DK	Rochdale
AO	Cumberland	BZ	Down	DL	Isle of Wight
AP	Sussex (East)			DM	Flintshire
AR	Hertfordshire	C	Yorkshire	DN	York
AS	Nairnshire	CA	Denbighshire	DO	Lincolnshire
AT	Kingston-upon-	CB	Blackburn		(Holland)
	Hull	CC	Caernarvonshire	DP	Reading
AU	Nottingham	CD	Brighton	DR	Plymouth
AV	Aberdeenshire	CE	Cambridgeshire	DS	Peeblesshire
AW	Salop	CF	Suffolk (West)	DT	Doncaster
AX	Monmouthshire	CG	Hampshire	DU	Coventry
AY	Leicestershire	CH	Derby	DV	Devon
AZ	Belfast	CI	Laoighis	DW	Newport (Mon.)
		CJ	Herefordshire	DX	Ipswich
B	Lancashire	CK	Preston	DY	Hastings
BA	Salford	CL	Norwich	DZ	Antrim
BB	Newcastle upon	CM	Birkenhead		
	Tyne	CN	Gateshead	E	Staffordshire
BC	Leicester	CO	Plymouth	EA	West Bromwich
BD	Northampton-	CP	Halifax	EB	Cambridge
	shire	CR	Southampton	EC	Westmorland
BE	Lincolnshire	CS	Ayrshire	ED	Warrington
	(Lindsey)	CT	Lincolnshire	EE	Grimsby
BF	Staffordshire		(Kesteven)	EF	West Hartlepool
BG	Birkenhead	CU	South Shields	EG	Huntingdon
BH	Buckingham-	CV	Cornwall	EH	Stoke-on-Trent
	shire	CW	Burnley	EI	Sligo
BI	Monaghan	CX	Huddersfield	EJ	Cardiganshire
BJ	Suffolk (East)	CY	Swansea	EK	Wigan
BK	Portsmouth	CZ	Belfast	EL	Bournemouth
BL	Berkshire			EM	Bootle
BM	Bedfordshire	D	Kent	EN	Bury
BN	Bolton	DA	Wolverhampton	EO	Barrow-in-Furness
BO	Cardiff	DB	Stockport	EP	Montgomeryshire
BP	Sussex (West)	DC	Middlesbrough	ER	Cambridgeshire
BR	Sunderland	DD	Gloucestershire	ES	Perthshire
BS	Orkney	DE	Pembrokeshire	ET	Rotherham

EU	Breconshire	GF	London	HV	London
EV	Essex	GG	Glasgow	HW	Bristol
EW	Huntingdonshire	GH	London	HX	London
EX	Great Yarmouth	GJ	London	HY	Bristol
EY	Anglesey	GK	London	HZ	Tyrone
EZ	Belfast	GL	Bath		
		GM	Motherwell and		
F	Essex		Wishaw	IA	Antrim
FA	Burton-on-Trent	GN	London	IB	Armagh
FB	Bath	GO	London	IC	Carlow
FC	Oxford	GP	London	ID	Cavan
FD	Dudley	GR	Sunderland	IE	Clare
FE	Lincoln	GS	Perthshire	IF	Cork
FF	Merionethshire	GT	London	IH	Donegal
FG	Fife	GU	London	IJ	Down
FH	Gloucester	GV	Suffolk (West)	IK	City and County
FI	Tipperary	GW	London		of Dublin
FJ	Exeter	GX	London	IL	Fermanagh
FK	Worcester	GY	London	IM	Galway
FL	Huntingdon	GZ	Belfast	IN	Kerry
FM	Chester			IO	Kildare
FN	Canterbury	H	London	IP	Kilkenny
FO	Radnorshire	HA	Warley	IR	Offaly
FP	Rutland	HB	Merthyr Tydfil	IT	Leitrim
FR	Blackpool	HC	Eastbourne	IU	Limerick
FS	Edinburgh	HD	Dewsbury	IW	Londonderry
FT	Tynemouth	HE	Barnsley	IX	Longford
FU	Lincolnshire	HF	Wallasey	IY	Louth
	(Lindsey)	HG	Burnley	IZ	Mayo
FV	Blackpool	HH	Carlisle		
FW	Lincolnshire	HI	Tipperary	J	Durham
	(Lindsey)	HJ	Southend	JA	Stockport
FX	Dorset	HK	Essex	JB	Berkshire
FY	Southport	HL	Wakefield	JC	Caernarvonshire
FZ	Belfast	HM	London	JD	London
		HN	Darlington	JE	Cambridge
G	Glasgow	HO	Hampshire	JF	Leicester
GA	Glasgow	HP	Coventry	JG	Canterbury
GB	Glasgow	HR	Wiltshire	JH	Hertfordshire
GC	London	HS	Renfrewshire	JI	Tyrone
GD	Glasgow	HT	Bristol	JJ	London
GE	Glasgow	HU	Bristol	JK	Eastbourne

JL	Lincolnshire (Holland)	KX	Buckingham-shire	MI	Wexford
JM	Westmorland	KY	Bradford	MJ	Bedfordshire
JN	Southend	KZ	Antrim	MK	London
JO	Oxford			ML	London
JP	Wigan			MM	London
JR	Northumber-land	L	Glamorgan	MN	Isle of Man
		LA	London	MO	Berkshire
JS	Ross and Cromarty	LB	London	MP	London
		LC	London	MR	Wiltshire
JT	Dorset	LD	London	MS	Stirlingshire
JU	Leicestershire	LE	London	MT	London
JV	Grimsby	LF	London	MU	London
JW	Wolverhampton	LG	Cheshire	MV	London
JX	Halifax	LH	London	MW	Wiltshire
JY	Plymouth	LI	Westmeath	MX	London
JZ	Down	LJ	Bournemouth	MY	London
		LK	London	MZ	Belfast
K	Liverpool	LL	London		
KA	Liverpool	LM	London	N	Manchester
KB	Liverpool	LN	London	NA	Manchester
KC	Liverpool	LO	London	NB	Manchester
KD	Liverpool	LP	London	NC	Manchester
KE	Kent	LR	London	ND	Manchester
KF	Liverpool	LS	Selkirkshire	NE	Manchester
KG	Cardiff	LT	London	NF	Manchester
KH	Kingston-upon-Hull	LU	London	NG	Norfolk
		LV	Liverpool	NH	Northampton
KI	Waterford	LW	London	NI	Wicklow
KJ	Kent	LX	London	NJ	Sussex (East)
KK	Kent	LY	London	NK	Hertfordshire
KL	Kent	LZ	Armagh	NL	Northumberland
KM	Kent			NM	Bedfordshire
KN	Kent	M	Cheshire	NN	Nottinghamshire
KO	Kent	MA	Cheshire	NO	Essex
KP	Kent	MB	Cheshire	NP	Worcestershire
KR	Kent	MC	London	NR	Leicestershire
KS	Roxburghshire	MD	London	NS	Sutherland
KT	Kent	ME	London	NT	Salop
KU	Bradford	MF	London	NU	Derbyshire
KV	Coventry	MG	London	NV	Northamptonshire
KW	Bradford	MH	London	NW	Leeds
				NX	Warwickshire

NY	Glamorgan	PL	Surrey	RL	Cornwall
NZ	Londonderry	PM	Sussex (East)	RM	Cumberland
		PN	Sussex (East)	RN	Preston
O	Birmingham	PO	Sussex (West)	RO	Hertfordshire
OA	Birmingham	PP	Buckingham-	RP	Northamptonshire
OB	Birmingham		shire	RR	Nottinghamshire
OC	Birmingham	PR	Dorset	RS	Aberdeen
OD	Devon	PS	Shetland	RT	Suffolk (East)
OE	Birmingham		(Zetland)	RU	Bournemouth
OF	Birmingham	PT	Durham	RV	Portsmouth
OG	Birmingham		(County)	RW	Coventry
OH	Birmingham	PU	Essex	RX	Berkshire
OI	Belfast	PV	Ipswich	RY	Leicester
OJ	Birmingham	PW	Norfolk	RZ	Antrim
OK	Birmingham	PX	Sussex (West)		
OL	Birmingham	PY	Yorkshire	S	Edinburgh
OM	Birmingham	PZ	Belfast	SA	Aberdeenshire
ON	Birmingham			SB	Argyll
OO	Essex			SC	Edinburgh
OP	Birmingham	QA QJ	London:	SD	Ayrshire
OR	Hampshire	QB QK	for	SE	Banffshire
OS	Wigtownshire	QC QL	vehicles	SF	Edinburgh
OT	Hampshire	QD QM	temporarily	SG	Edinburgh
OU	Hampshire	QE QN	imported	SH	Berwickshire
OV	Birmingham	QF QP	from	SJ	Bute
OW	Southampton	QG QQ	abroad	SK	Caithness
OX	Birmingham	QH QS		SL	Clackmannan-
OY	London				shire
OZ	Belfast	R	Derbyshire	SM	Dumfriesshire
		RA	Derbyshire	SN	Dunbartonshire
P	Surrey	RB	Derbyshire	SO	Moray
PA	Surrey	RC	Derby	SP	Fife
PB	Surrey	RD	Reading	SR	Angus
PC	Surrey	RE	Staffordshire	SS	East Lothian
PD	Surrey	RF	Staffordshire	ST	Inverness-shire
PE	Surrey	RG	Aberdeen	SU	Kincardineshire
PF	Surrey	RH	Kingston-upon-	SV	Kinross-shire
PG	Surrey		Hull	SW	Kirkcudbright-
PH	Surrey	RI	City and County		shire
PI	Cork		of Dublin	SX	West Lothian
PJ	Surrey	RJ	Salford	SY	Midlothian
PK	Surrey	RK	London	SZ	Down

T	Devon	UL	London	VZ	Tyrone
TA	Devon	UM	Leeds		
TB	Lancashire	UN	Denbighshire		
TC	Lancashire	UO	Devon	W	Sheffield
TD	Lancashire	UP	Durham	WA	Sheffield
TE	Lancashire		(County)	WB	Sheffield
TF	Lancashire	UR	Hertfordshire	WC	Essex
TG	Glamorgan	US	Glasgow	WD	Warwickshire
TH	Carmarthenshire	UT	Leicestershire	WE	Sheffield
TI	Limerick	UU	London	WF	Yorkshire
TJ	Lancashire	UV	London	WG	Stirlingshire
TK	Dorset	UW	London	WH	Bolton
TL	Lincolnshire	UX	Salop	WI	Waterford
	(Kesteven)	UY	Worcestershire	WJ	Sheffield
TM	Bedfordshire	UZ	Belfast	WK	Coventry
TN	Newcastle upon			WL	Oxford
	Tyne	V	Lanarkshire	WM	Southport
TO	Nottingham	VA	Lanarkshire	WN	Swansea
TP	Portsmouth	VB	London	WO	Monmouthshire
TR	Southampton	VC	Coventry	WP	Worcestershire
TS	Dundee	VD	Lanarkshire	WR	Yorkshire
TT	Devon	VE	Cambridgeshire	WS	Edinburgh
TU	Cheshire	VF	Norfolk	WT	Yorkshire
TV	Nottingham	VG	Norwich	WU	Yorkshire
TW	Essex	VH	Huddersfield	WV	Wiltshire
TX	Glamorgan	VJ	Herefordshire	WW	Yorkshire
TY	Northumber-	VK	Newcastle upon	WX	Yorkshire
	land		Tyne	WY	Yorkshire
TZ	Belfast	VL	Lincoln	WZ	Belfast
		VM	Manchester		
U	Leeds	VN	Yorkshire	X	Northumberland
UA	Leeds	VO	Nottingham-	XA	London
UB	Leeds		shire	XB	London
UC	London	VP	Birmingham	XC	London
UD	Oxfordshire	VR	Manchester	XD	London
UE	Warwickshire	VS	Greenock	XE	London
UF	Brighton	VT	Stoke-on-Trent	XF	London
UG	Leeds	VU	Manchester	XG	Middlesbrough
UH	Cardiff	VV	Northampton	XH	London
UI	Londonderry	VW	Essex	XI	Belfast
UJ	Salop	VX	Essex	XJ	Manchester
UK	Wolverhampton	VY	York	XK	London

XL	London	Y	Somerset	YM	London
XM	London	YA	Somerset	YN	London
XN	London	YB	Somerset	YO	London
XO	London	YC	Somerset	YP	London
XP	London	YD	Somerset	YR	London
XR	London	YE	London	YS	Glasgow
XS	Paisley	YF	London	YT	London
XT	London	YG	Yorkshire	YU	London
XU	London	YH	London	YV	London
XV	London	YI	City and County	YW	London
XW	London		of Dublin	YX	London
XX	London	YJ	Dundee	YY	London
XY	London	YK	London	YZ	Londonderry
XZ	Armagh	YL	London		

A	City and County of Dublin	ZM	Galway
ZA	City and County of Dublin	ZN	Meath
ZB	Cork (County)	ZO	City and County of Dublin
ZC	City and County of Dublin	ZP	Donegal
ZD	City and County of Dublin	ZR	Wexford
ZE	City and County of Dublin	ZT	Cork (County)
ZF	Cork	ZU	City and County of Dublin
ZH	City and County of Dublin	ZW	Kildare
ZI	City and County of Dublin	ZX	Kerry
ZJ	City and County of Dublin	ZY	Louth
ZK	Cork (County)	ZZ	Dublin: for vehicles temp-
ZL	City and County of Dublin		orarily imported from abroad

International Registration Letters

A	Austria	BR	Brazil
ADN	Southern Yemen (formerly Aden)	BRG	Guyana (formerly British Guiana)
AL	Albania	BRN	Bahrain
AND	Andorra	BRU	Brunei
AUS	Australia	BS	Bahamas
B	Belgium	BUR	Burma
BDS	Barbados	C	Cuba
BG	Bulgaria	CDN	Canada
BH	British Honduras	CGO	Zaire

CH	Switzerland	IL	Israel
CI	Ivory Coast	IND	India
CL	Sri Lanka (Ceylon)	IR	Iran
CO	Colombia	IRL	Ireland (Republic of)
CR	Costa Rica	IRQ	Iraq
CS	Czechoslovakia	IS	Iceland
CY	Cyprus	J	Japan
D	Germany	JA	Jamaica
DK	Denmark	K	Cambodia
DOM	Dominican Republic	KWT	Kuwait
DY	Dahomey	L	Luxembourg
DZ	Algeria	LAO	Laos
E	Spain (incl. African	LB	Liberia
	localities and provinces)	LS	Lesotho (formerly
EAK	Kenya		Basutoland)
EAT	Tanzania (formerly	M	Malta
	Tanganyika)	MA	Morocco
EAU	Uganda	MC	Monaco
EAZ	Tanzania (formerly	MEX	Mexico
	Zanzibar)	MS	Mauritius
EC	Ecuador	MW	Malawi (formerly
ET	United Arab Republic		Nyasaland)
	(Egypt)	N	Norway
F	France (incl. overseas	NA	Netherlands Antilles
	departments and	NIC	Nicaragua
	territories)	NIG	Niger
FL	Liechtenstein	NL	Netherlands
GB	United Kingdom of Great	NZ	New Zealand
	Britain and Northern	P	Portugal (incl. Angola,
	Ireland		Cape Verde Islands,
GBA	Alderney ⎫ Channel		Mozambique, Portuguese
GBG	Guernsey ⎬ Islands		Guinea, Portuguese
GBJ	Jersey ⎭		Timor, São Tomé and
GBM	Isle of Man		Príncipe)
GBZ	Gibraltar	PA	Panama
GCA	Guatemala	PAK	Pakistan
GH	Ghana	PE	Peru
GR	Greece	PI	Philippines
H	Hungary	PL	Poland
HK	Hong Kong	PTM	Malaysia
HKJ	Jordan	PY	Paraguay
I	Italy	R	Rumania

RA	Argentina	SN	Senegal
RB	Botswana (formerly Bechuanaland)	SU	Union of Soviet Socialist Republics
RC	China (National Republic) (Formosa)	SUD	Sudan
		SWA	South West Africa
RCA	Central African Republic	SY	Seychelles
RCB	Congo (Brazzaville)	SYR	Syria
RCH	Chile	T	Thailand
RH	Haiti	TG	Togo
RI	Indonesia	TN	Tunisia
RIM	Mauritania	TR	Turkey
RL	Lebanon	TT	Trinidad and Tobago
RM	Malagasy Republic (formerly Madagascar)	U	Uruguay
		USA	United States of America
RMM	Mali	V	Vatican City (Holy See)
RNR	Zambia (formerly Northern Rhodesia)	VN	Vietnam (Republic of)
		WAG	Gambia
ROK	Korea (Republic of)	WAL	Sierra Leone
RSM	San Marino	WAN	Nigeria
RSR	Rhodesia (formerly Southern Rhodesia)	WD	Dominica ⎫
		WG	Grenada ⎬ Windward Islands
RU	Burundi	WL	St Lucia ⎭
RWA	Rwanda	WS	Western Samoa
S	Sweden	WV	St Vincent (Windward Islands)
SD	Swaziland		
SF	Finland	YU	Yugoslavia
SGP	Singapore	YV	Venezuela
SME	Surinam (Dutch Guiana)	ZA	South Africa

Some Important Dates in the Story of Motoring

1770 Nicholas Cugnot built a 3-wheeled steam wagon – the first real automobile in the sense that it moved under its own steam.

1801 Richard Trevithick, a Cornishman, built Britain's first steam carriage. He later concentrated on steam locomotives (see p. 112).

1835 The Highways Act largely superseded the Turnpike Acts. It created the offence of 'Riding or driving furiously so as to endanger the life or limb of any person'.

1861 The Locomotives Act required all motor vehicles to be in the charge of two people and imposed a speed limit of 10 mph in the country and 5 mph in towns.

1865 The Locomotives Act imposed a 4 mph speed limit (2 mph in towns) and required a crew of three for all mechanically propelled vehicles, stipulating that one of the crew must walk not less than 6 yards in front carrying a red flag by day and a lantern by night.

1878 The red flag was abolished but one member of the crew was required to walk in front to warn horsemen – at a distance of 20 yards.

1885 Two German engineers – Gottlieb Daimler and Karl Benz – separately achieved the first practical results in the design of the horseless carriage which was to become the internal combustion motor car.

1892 The first petrol-engined car – an 1888 Benz – is thought to have been imported into Britain.

1894 Road racing started in France.
The *Petit Journal* inspired the 80-mile Paris-Rouen contest – the world's first open-road reliability trial.

1895 The Automobile Club de France was formed.
Michelin of France produced the first practical motor-car tyre.
The Paris-Bordeaux there-and-back 732 mile race was won by a Panhard-Levassor at 14·9 mph.
Britain's first motor show was organized at Tunbridge Wells.

1896 Dr Frederick Lanchester tested his four-wheeled, petrol-engined phaeton.
In the US Henry Ford built his first car – a quadri-cycle.
It became no longer necessary for a crew member to walk in front of the vehicle. Speeds of up to 14 mph were allowed. The passing of this Act was celebrated by the famous Emancipation Run from London to Brighton.

1897 Frederick Richard Simms – described as the 'father' of the British motor industry – founded the Automobile Club of Great Britain and Ireland (to become the RAC on December 8th).

1900 First of the Gordon Bennett races – the forerunners of the international Grand Prix races we know today.

1903 The Motor Car Act 1903 was passed. It was called the Motorist's Charter, and lifted the speed limit from 14 to 20 mph, provided for driving licences, compulsory registration and number plates.
Henry Ford set up a new world speed record at 91·37 mph in an Arrow.

1905 The Automobile Association was formed in June.
Herbert Austin founded the Austin Motor Co and produced the first Austin the following year.

The first Tourist Trophy race, in the Isle of Man, was won at 33·9 mph by Mr J. S. Napier in an Arrol-Johnston.

1907   The Rolls-Royce Silver Ghost made its first appearance. The 7,434 cc Ghost remained in production until 1925.
On June 17th Brooklands racing track was opened near Weybridge, Surrey. In July Selwyn Edge used it to set up a 24-hour record in a Napier, completing 1,582 miles at an average speed of close on 66 mph.

1908   Birth of the Model T Ford – the 'Tin Lizzie' with its 2,880 cc engine and 2-speed epicyclic gearbox.

1910   Petrol tax was introduced at 3d a gallon. A graduated scale of motor licence duties was introduced.

1919   First post-war Motor Show. Motorists were paying 4s a gallon for petrol which had cost 1s 9d before the war.

1920   Britain's first roadside petrol pump was installed at Aldermaston, near Newbury, Berks.

1922   Herbert Austin introduced his 747 cc Baby Austin with three-speed gearbox and four-wheel brakes.

1923   Henry Seagrave, in a Sunbeam, gained Britain's first Grand Prix victory.

1930   Abolition of the 20 mph speed limit.

1934   New Road Traffic Act imposed a 30 mph speed limit in built-up areas which came into operation the following year.
Driving licence tests introduced.

1935   Malcolm Campbell, in his Rolls-engined Bluebird, raised the land-speed record above the 300 mph mark for the first time (301·13 mph).

1937   London Motor Show held for the first time at Earl's Court.

1938   The number of motor vehicles on Britain's roads exceeded 3,000,000 for the first time.

1939   John Cobb in his car 'Railton' set up a new world land-speed record of 369·7 mph. Petrol rationing introduced.

1942   Basic petrol ration withdrawn.

1947   On Bonneville Salt Flats, Utah, John Cobb pushed the world land-speed record to 394·2 mph (Sept. 16th). On one of his runs he exceeded 400 mph on land – a record which remained unbeaten for 17 years.

1950   Petrol rationing abolished on July 1st. The tubeless tyre perfected in the USA.

1955   Britain's first Highway Code.

1956   The Road Traffic Act 1956 included a compulsory annual test for vehicles ten years old or more.

1958 Britain's first stretch of motorway opened – the Preston By-Pass (Dec. 5th). First parking meter order made.

1960 The Road Traffic and Roads Improvement Act 1960 provided for the appointment of Traffic Wardens by the Police. The start of motor vehicle testing on a voluntary basis at more than 14,000 testing stations.

1964 On Lake Eyre, S. Australia, Donald Campbell in his wheel-driven car 'Bluebird' achieved a speed of 429·311 mph over 666·386 yards. Peak speed: *c.* 440 mph.

1965 Craig Breedlove set up an official speed of 608·21 mph in four-wheeled jet-propelled car 'The Spirit of America' at Bonneville Salt Flats, Utah, on Nov. 15th.

1967 The breath test introduced: motorists in Great Britain subject to a legal maximum limit to the amount of alcohol which they may have in their blood.

1968 Introduction of tests for heavy goods vehicles.

1969 Cars first registered on or after January 1st 1965, are required to have safety belts in front seats – later cars must already have seat belts.

1971 Minimum age for riding motor cycles, scooters or three-wheelers raised from 16 to 17.

1972 Motorway mileage in Britain reached 1,000 miles.

1973 Compulsory wearing of safety helmets for riders of two-wheeled motor cycles became law.

1974 VAT on petrol (at 10%) introduced for the first time – within a few months it was reduced to 8% and then, in the same year, raised to 25%. The average cost of a gallon of petrol soared from 42p at the beginning of the year to 76p at the close.

1975 VASCAR – a new speed trap device – came into general use following successful tests which began in 1971 in Essex.

1976 Introduction of Driving Licences for Life. VAT on petrol reduced to 12%, Fuel Tax up 7½p to 30p a gallon.

C. Railways

Fastest Individual Runs in Great Britain

THE CURRENT BRITISH STEAM TRAIN RECORD is held by the steam locomotive 'Mallard' which hauled 7 coaches weighing 240 tons at 126 mph for 440 yards between Grantham and Peterborough on July 3rd, 1938.

THE CURRENT BRITISH AND WORLD DIESEL TRAIN RECORD is held by the 'High Speed Train' which consisted of 2 power cars and 6 coaches weighing 326 tons and travelled at 143 mph for one mile between Thirsk and Tollerton on June 12th, 1973.

THE FASTEST REGULAR RAILWAY RUN IN THE WORLD is the 'New Tokaido' service of the Japanese National Railways inaugurated on March 15th, 1972. The train covers the 100 miles from Osaka to Okayama in 58 minutes, averaging 103·875 mph.

THE LONGEST DAILY NON-STOP RUN IN THE WORLD is made by the 'Florida Special', between New York City and Miami, a distance of 1,377 miles.

THE FASTEST REGULAR RUN ON BRITISH RAIL is the 65-mile stretch from Rugby to Watford in 44 minutes.

THE LONGEST RUN ON BRITISH RAIL without an advertised stop is the 'Night Aberdonian' from King's Cross to Inverkeithing, a distance of 406¼ miles.

THE WORLD'S LONGEST STRETCH OF ELECTRIFIED LINE is the 4,000 miles between Moscow, Baikal and Karimskaya, in Siberia, USSR, completed in 1973.

MONORAIL. THE HIGHEST SPEED EVER ATTAINED ON RAILS is 3,090 mph (Mach 4·1) by an unmanned, rocket-powered sled at New Mexico, USA. It is hoped to attain speeds of 608 mph (Mach 0·8) from a wheel-less, rocket-powered train running on rollers and designed by Professor H. Ozawa (Japan).

Some Important Dates in the Story of Railways in Britain

1801, May 21st – Incorporation of the Surrey Iron Railway, the first public goods line in the world to be sanctioned by Parliament. Opened from Wandsworth to Croydon on July 16th, 1803.

1804, February 21st – Steam locomotive traction successfully used (experimentally) by Trevithick on the Penydaran tramroad at Merthyr Tydfil. **June 29th** – Incorporation of Oystermouth Railway or Tramroad Company, the first to convey fare-paying passengers. The line from Swansea to Oystermouth, opened in 1806, was worked successively by horse, steam and electricity.

1814, July 25th – George Stephenson's first locomotive, '*Blücher*', introduced on the Killingworth Colliery wagonway.

1825, September 27th – Ceremonial opening of Stockton and Darlington Railway. Stephenson's locomotive '*Locomotion*' reached 15 mph.

1829, October 6th–14th – Trials on the Rainhill Level (Liverpool and Manchester Railway): Stephenson's '*Rocket*' won first prize of £500.

1830, September 15th – Liverpool and Manchester Railway formally opened, the first public railway in the world to be worked entirely by steam locomotives. This day also marked the first railway accident. William Huskisson, MP, was run down by Stephenson's '*Rocket*' and died the same night.

1836, April 20th – Festiniog Railway (1 ft. 11½ in. gauge) opened for slate traffic. The first narrow gauge public railway in the world.

1837, July 4th – Grand Junction Railway opened throughout – the first British trunk railway.

1842, June 13th – First railway journey made by Queen Victoria – from Slough to Paddington.

1845, August 6th – Opening of the Gauge Commission. Decision in favour of 4 ft. 8½ in. gauge as British standard reached the next year, with the exception of GWR and associated lines.

1854, January 16th – Present Paddington station opened, Great Western Railway.

1855, February 1st – GWR inaugurated the first special postal train in the world between London and Bristol. One first-class carriage was attached for passengers in June 1869.

1857 – First steel rail made (by Robert Forester Mushet) and laid experimentally at Derby Station, Midland Railway, early in 1857. It remained in service until June 1873, and steel rails came into general use a few years later.

1863, January 10th – First underground city railway in the world opened, on the Metropolitan Railway, from Bishop's Road to Farringdon Street.

1868, October 1st – St Pancras Station opened, Midland Railway.

1874, February 2nd – Liverpool Street Station opened, Great Eastern Railway.

June 1st – Pullman cars introduced to Great Britain by Midland Railway.

1877, December – Sleeping cars (1st class) introduced on GWR.

1879, November 1st – Dining-car introduced on Great Northern Railway, London–Leeds service.

1883, August 4th – First section of Magnus Volk's Brighton electric railway opened. Pioneer electric railway in Great Britain.

September 28th – Electric traction formally inaugurated on the Giant's Causeway Railway. The first line in the world to be run on hydro-electric power.

1890, December 18th – City and South London Railway opened. First underground electric railway in the world.

1892, March 7th – Corridor trains introduced on GWR services.

1905, September 12th – Electric traction inaugurated on Inner Circle.

1921, August 19th – Royal Assent given to the Railways Act 1921 which resulted in the formation of the four British main-line railway companies.

1926, September 12th – The 'Golden Arrow' all-Pullman service, Calais–Paris, introduced on the through London–Paris route.

1933, January 1st – The '*Southern Belle*' – the first all-steel, all-electric Pullman train in the world, introduced by Southern Railway (re-named '*Brighton Belle*' on June 29th, 1934).

1935, September 27th – Trial run of LNER '*Silver Jubilee*' (London–Newcastle express) the first streamlined train in Great Britain. Attained an average speed of 100 mph for 43 miles.

1937, June 29th – Trial run of LMSR '*Coronation Scot*' streamlined express (London–Glasgow). Maximum speed of 114 mph attained approaching Crewe. Public service began July 5th.

1948, January 1st – British Railways nationalized.

1961, September 9th – Last day of steam haulage of regular passenger service on the Metropolitan Line, London Transport.

1963, March 27th – Dr Richard Beeching's report on the re-shaping of British Railways published. Among the main proposals: 2,128 of Britain's 7,000 stations and halts to be closed; passenger train services to be completely withdrawn from about 5,000 route miles; and many stopping passenger services to be discontinued.

April 8th – First London Transport train fitted with automatic driving equipment entered experimental service on District line.

1965, June 11th – The last regular booked steam passenger train left Paddington. This marked the end of steam at Paddington except for special workings: the last was on November 27th. The official title of British Railways is, in fact, still British Railways, but from 1965 onwards the normal usage became 'British Rail'.

1966, July 5th – Opening of British Railways '*Seaspeed*' hovercraft service between Southampton and Cowes.

1968, August – Opening of '*Seaspeed*' hovercraft service between Dover and Boulogne. Service later extended to Calais.

1968, October 14th – Queen Elizabeth II formally opened the rebuilt Euston Station, London.

1969, March 7th – Victoria Line, London Transport, opened throughout from Walthamstow to Victoria by Queen Elizabeth II – the first new tube across central London for over half a century and the most highly automated Underground railway line in the world.

1972, February – Work started on the first section of the Fleet Line deep-level 'tube' railway, London Transport.

1972, July 25th – A P T (Advanced Passenger Train) took to the rails for the first time.

1973, June – High Speed train breaks British train speed record by reaching 131 mph; and breaks world diesel train speed record by reaching 143 mph.

1973, June – Announcement of introduction of first 5,000 horsepower electric locomotive for British Rail.

1974, May 6th – The London–Glasgow record over 391 miles was set at 4 hours 58 minutes by the *Royal Scot*.

1975, June – Advanced Passenger Train ran at 152 mph on Western Region main line, setting up a British Rail speed record.

1975, August 27th – National Railway Museum opened at York.

D. Aircraft

British Airways

The British Airways Board was established in 1972 to control all the activities of British European Airways (BEA) and British Overseas Airways Corporation (BOAC), to review the organization of the state sector of British civil air transport, to report to the Secretary of State on what changes, if any, were required and with all the necessary powers to operate air transport services and to do all other forms of aerial work, worldwide, on its own account.

Since 1st April, 1974, the two state air corporations (BEA and BOAC) have been dissolved, and the new group now trades under the name of 'British Airways'.

The Group has seven operating divisions, each with its own commercial and marketing integrity.

British Airways has 191 aircraft, total assets of over £500 million and annual revenues of more than £800 million, over half of which is earned overseas. The airline is one of the world's biggest carriers of international air traffic and has the world's biggest and most comprehensive route network.

British Airways Fact Sheet

British Airways Operational Fleet (as at 5 May 1976)

Aircraft types			
		BAC1–11	25
	(Helicopter)	Bell Jetranger	1
	(Helicopter)	Bell 212	1
		Boeing 707	24 (3 all cargo)
		Boeing 747	18
		Concorde	2
		HS 748	2
		Merchantman	5 (all cargo)
	(Helicopter)	S58T	2
	(Helicopter)	Sikorsky 61N	13
		Trident 1 & 1-E	13
		Trident 2	15
		Trident 3	26
		TriStar	7

VC10
  (Standard)   2
VC10 (Super) 15
Viscounts   20
(On Order: 4 Boeing 747; 3 Concorde; 8 Lockheed TriStar)

Destinations	164 in 78 countries
Total Route Network	Approx 500,000 miles
Revenue Passengers (April 1st 1975 *on* March 31st 1976)	13,792,000
Total Number of Employees Worldwide	57,000

Badges of Rank of Officers of The Royal Air Force

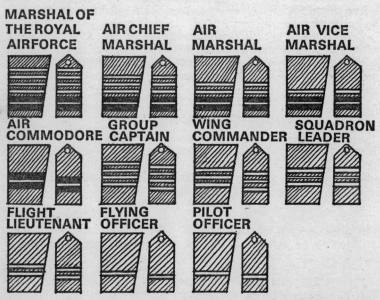

MARSHAL OF THE ROYAL AIRFORCE

AIR CHIEF MARSHAL

AIR MARSHAL

AIR VICE MARSHAL

AIR COMMODORE

GROUP CAPTAIN

WING COMMANDER

SQUADRON LEADER

FLIGHT LIEUTENANT

FLYING OFFICER

PILOT OFFICER

The principal non-commissioned ranks are: Warrant Officer, Flight Sergeant (Flt Sgt), Chief Technician (Chief Tech), Sergeant (Sgt), Corporal (Cpl), Junior Technician (Jnr. Tech), Senior Aircraftman (SAC), Leading Aircraftman (LAC), Aircraftman (AC).

Some Famous British Aircraft of World War II

Spitfire (fighter). Low-wing monoplane. The 'Spit' played a great part in defeating the Luftwaffe in the Battle of Britain.
Max. speed: 375 mph at 20,250 ft.
Span: 36 ft. 10 in.; Length: 30 ft. 4 in.

Hurricane (fighter-light bomber). Low-wing monoplane with single in-line engine. Played an outstanding role in the Battle of Britain. Hurricanes shot down more aircraft than all other types put together.
Approx speed: 335 mph at 22,000 ft.
Span: 40 ft.; Length: 31 ft. 5 in.

Wellington (medium bomber). Twin-engined, mid-wing monoplane. One of the most-used British bombers, known as the 'Wimpy'. The Wellington II had in-line engines; Wellington III, radial engines.
Approx. max. speed: 244 mph at 17,000 ft.
Span: 86 ft. 2 in.; Length: 61 ft. (II), 61 ft. 6 in. (III).
Range: 3,240 miles.

Stirling (heavy bomber). Mid-wing monoplane with four radial engines. Inboard engines underslung. First of the big British four-engined bombers to go into service, becoming operational early in 1941. Carried over 8 tons of bombs.
Approx. max. speed: 272 mph at 14,000 ft.
Span: 99 ft.; Length: 87 ft. 3 in.

Halifax (heavy bomber). Mid-wing monoplane with four in-line engines underslung. Pilots called it the 'Halibag'. Its 'block-busting' bombs caused considerable damage in Germany and the Middle East. Max. bomb load approx. 11,000 lb.
Max. speed: 262 mph at 17,750 ft.
Span: 99 ft.; Length: 71 ft. 7 in.

Lancaster (heavy bomber). Mid-wing monoplane. Four in-line engines underslung. The 'dam-busters' bomber: carried a bomb load of over 6 tons.
Max. speed: 280 mph.
Span: 102 ft.; Length: 69 ft. 6 in.
Range: nearly 3,000 miles.

Sunderland. Four-engined flying boat nicknamed the 'Flying Porcupine' due to its many guns. Armed with power-operated turrets in the nose and in the tail; the tail turret carried 4 guns. Two flank gun positions each carried a single machine gun. Especially concerned with coastal reconnaissance, convoying ships and in submarine patrol. Loaded weight: 44,600 lb.

Mosquito (light bomber-fighter). Twin engine, high mid-wing monoplane. Reconnaissance bomber. Constructed for the most part of plywood. Became operational at the end of 1942.
Span: 54 ft. 2 in.; Length: 40 ft. 9½ in.

Swordfish (torpedo bomber). Single radial engine biplane with fabric-covered wings, used by the British Fleet Air Arm for torpedo, spotter and reconnaissance work. Carried either a load of bombs or a single 18-inch torpedo slung between the divided undercarriage legs.
Max. speed: 144 mph at 5,500 ft.
Span: 45 ft. 6 in.; Length: 36 ft. 4 in.

Blenheim (medium bomber). Mid-wing monoplane with twin radial engines, used as a bomber and long-range fighter over France, in the North African campaigns and in the Middle East.
Max. speed: 260 mph at 12,000 ft.
Span: 56 ft.; Length: 42 ft. 7 in.

Some Important Dates in the History of Flying

1783, October 15th – François Pilâtre de Rozier became the world's first aeronaut when he ascended 84 feet above Paris in a hot-air balloon designed by Joseph and Etienne Montgolfier.

1903, December 17th – Orville and Wilbur Wright made the first sustained controlled flights in history in a powered aeroplane, the 'Flyer', at Kitty Hawk, N. Carolina, covering 120 feet in about 12 seconds.

1908, October 16th – Samuel F. Cody made the first officially recognized aeroplane flight in Great Britain, at Farnborough, Hants.

1909, July 25th – Louis Bleriot of France crossed the English Channel in a Bleriot XI monoplane. He took off from Baraques, near Calais, at 4.40 AM and landed at Dover at 5.20 AM.

1912 (mid-August) – F. K. McClean flew a Short pusher biplane under all the Thames bridges in London between Tower Bridge and Westminster, passing between the upper and lower spans of Tower Bridge.

1913, August 20th – Lt Nesterov, of the Imperial Russian Army, first looped-the-loop in a Nieuport at Kiev.

1913 – Appearance of the first four-engined aeroplane in the world – the Sikorsky 'Grand'.

1918, April 1st – The Royal Air Force was formed.

1919, June 14th–15th – Capt John Alcock and Lt Arthur Whitten Brown made the first non-stop air crossing of the Atlantic in a Vickers Vimy bomber from St John's, Newfoundland to Clifden, Co Galway, Ireland.

1919, November 12th–December 10th – Two Australian brothers, Capt Ross Smith and Lt Keith Smith made the first flight from England to Australia – a distance of 11,294 miles.

1925–6, November 16th–March 12th – First flight from London to Cape Town and return by Alan Cobham in a de Havilland DH-50.

1926, June 30th–October 1st – First aeroplane flight from Britain to Australia and return made by Alan Cobham in a de Havilland DH-50. After this flight he was knighted.

1927, May 20th–21st – First solo non-stop crossing of the Atlantic by Capt Charles Lindbergh. New York to Paris – 33 hours 30 minutes.

1928, May 15th – The Australian Flying Doctor Service was inaugurated.

1929, August 8th–29th – First airship flight round the world. The Graf Zeppelin, commanded by Dr Hugo Eckener, flew from Lakehurst, New Jersey, to Friedrichshafen, Tokyo, Los Angeles and back to Lakehurst in 21 days, 7 hours, 34 minutes.

1929, November 28th–29th – Cdr R. E. Byrd made the first flight over the South Pole.

1930, May 5th–24th – First solo flight from England to Australia by a woman. Amy Johnson flew a de Havilland Moth from Croydon to Darwin in 19 days.

1930, October 4th – Airship R101 crashed in France on its maiden voyage, a disaster which put an end to airship development in Britain.

1932, August 18th–19th – First east to west crossing of the North Atlantic, by J. A. Mollison, in a de Havilland Puss Moth.

1933, July 15th–22nd – The first solo flight round the world. Wiley Post (American) flew a Lockheed monoplane from New York via Berlin, Moscow, Irkutsk, Alaska and back to New York – 15,596 miles in 7 days, 18 hours, 49 minutes.

1936, June 26th – The first prototype of the Focke-Wulf FW 61 twin-rotor helicopter made its first free flight – the first successful helicopter in the world.

1937, May 6th – The German Zeppelin '*Hindenburg*', then the world's largest airship, caught fire and was destroyed when approaching its moorings at Lakehurst, America, with the loss of 35 lives. Before this it had completed ten transatlantic flights carrying up to 100 passengers each time. The crossing took 62 hours.

1939, August 27th – The first jet-propelled aeroplane to fly was the German Heinkel He 178.

1940 (summer) – Fewer than 1,000 Hurricane and Spitfire fighters of the Royal Air Force met and defeated 3,500 aircraft of three Luftwaffe air fleets.

1941, October 2nd – A speed of 623 mph in level flight was recorded by Heini Dittmar in the Messerschmitt Me 163 '*Komet*' – the world's first operational rocket-powered fighter.

1947, October 14th – The first supersonic flight was made by Capt (now Lt-Gen) Charles E. Yeager, USAF, over Edwards Air Force Base, Muroc, California, USA, in a US Bell XS-I.

1950 – British European Airways commenced the first jet airliner service in the world – London-Le Bourget, in 57 minutes.

1952, May 2nd – The world's first jet airliner, a de Havilland Comet entered service (London-Johannesburg). Powered by four 4,450 lb. thrust turbojets. Cruising speed: 490 mph.

1953 – The world's first turboprop airliner service opened by British European Airways using 48-seat Vickers Viscounts. Four 1,540 hp Rolls-Royce Dart engines gave the early Viscount a cruising speed of 320 mph.

1957 – Russia puts first earth satellite, Sputnik 1, into orbit.

1967, October 3rd – The North American X-15A-2 fixed-wing rocket-powered research aircraft, which flew for the first time on 28th June 1964, reached a speed of 7,297 km/h (Mach 6·72).

1968 – Russia flies the world's first supersonic transport, the Tupolev Tu-144.

1969 – French and British prototype of the Concorde supersonic transport flown.

1970, January 12th – The Boeing 747 'Jumbo Jet' arrived in London from New York on its first passenger carrying flight. It takes from 362–490 passengers in ten-abreast rows. Cruising speed, 595 mph; wingspan: 195·7 ft.; length: 231·3 ft. Cost of each 747, £8¾m.

1974, September 13th – A British Caledonian Boeing 707 made the crossing from London to Los Angeles, covering seven time zones and 5,645 miles in 9 hours 38 minutes, breaking the speed record for passenger flights on this route.

1976, January 21st – Air France and British Airways inaugurated their supersonic Concorde services. The British Airways Concorde *Alpha Alpha* from Heathrow to Bahrain took 3 hours 37 minutes. Take-off time from Heathrow coincided with take-off of first Air France passenger service from Charles de Gaulle airport, Paris.

1976, May 24th – British Airways and Air France Concordes opened the supersonic era across the North Atlantic when they flew to Washington from London and Paris respectively in just under four hours – half the normal subsonic airliner time.

11 SPACE

Journey into Space

Cape Canaveral was once an arrowhead of land jutting into the ocean – a wasteland inhabited by insects, snakes and alligators.

Then, one day, the scientists, engineers and technicians moved in and built gantry towers, blockhouses and roads. And on July 24th, 1950, the first missile shot from Cape Canaveral blasted off and dropped into the Atlantic.

But the Space Age can really be said to have begun on October 4th, 1957, when the USSR successfully launched a 'sputnik' into orbit. Twelve years later, on July 21st, 1969, American astronaut Neil Armstrong became the first man to walk on the surface of the Moon. His words 'That's one small step for a man, one giant leap for mankind' have gone down in history – and America's £10,000,000,000 programme for landing a man on the Moon was crowned with success.

The total cost of manned spaceflight alone since the 1950s is in the region of $25,541,400,000. The estimated cost of the Space Shuttle programme to 1990 will be $2,800,000,000.

On June 22nd, 1973, three Skylab astronauts, Captain Charles 'Pete' Conrad, Dr Joseph P. Kerwin and Commander Paul J. Weitz splashed down in the Pacific at the end of a 28-day mission, setting a new record for space endurance. The previous record was 23 days, 18 hours, 22 minutes by the crew of the Russian Salyut-1 mission in 1971. The Skylab flight was plagued with problems. Just over an hour after Skylab was launched, a large, metal, heat-protection shield tore away. Later, a refrigeration system failed. All three astronauts experienced heart and circulatory trouble, with symptoms of nausea, dizziness and disorientation after splashdown. They recovered in a few days.

The Skylab programme has cost more than $2,500 million. Apollo spacecraft serve as ferry boats from Earth.

Skylab was 'home' to two other teams of astronauts in 1973. On September 27th Captain Alan Bean, Major Jack Lousma and Dr Owen Garriott returned to earth after 59½ days in Skylab 2; and on November 16th Gerald P. Carr, William R. Pogue and Edward Gibson splashed down after 85 days in Skylab 3.

Several unmanned attempts have been made by the Americans and Russians over the last ten years or so to reach Venus. The first 'official' Russian flight – Venus-1 – was launched in February 1961. Contact was lost and the flight was thought to have passed the planet. Another Soviet automatic spacecraft – Venus-7 – reached Venus on December 15th, 1970, after a flight lasting 120 days. It sent back signals to Earth for 23 minutes after landing before perishing in the intense heat of the planet's atmosphere. According to data relayed by the spacecraft the surface temperature in the landing area was about 887°F (475°C) and the density of the surface atmosphere was sixty times greater than that on Earth.

On March 27th, 1972, Russia soft-landed a new, instrumented, unmanned, one-ton probe, Venus 8, on the surface of that planet which transmitted information for 50 minutes before being destroyed by the conditions. Venus 9 and Venus 10 were launched, one after the other, on June 8th and June 14th, 1975.

Luna 24, Russia's unmanned Moon probe which landed in the Sea of Crises (August 1976) rocketed a sealed container of rock samples back towards Earth. The probe drilled a hole 7 feet deep to obtain the samples.

America's Mariner-9 spacecraft, the first spacecraft in history to orbit another planet, began circling Mars, after a 248-million mile journey from Cape Kennedy, on May 30th, 1971. It sent back invaluable information which is causing all previous scientific theories on the make-up and evolution of the planet to be drastically revised. In 1975 the Americans launched two unmanned spacecraft, Viking 1 and Viking 2, in readiness for the landing of robot-controlled automatic laboratories on the surface of Mars and the placing of scientific satellites in orbit around the planet.

In a most difficult technical operation, Viking 1 soft-landed under automatic control of its own computer brain on the Plain of Chryse on July 20th, 1976. Viking 2 landed on the Red Planet on September 4th, 1976, on the Plain of Utopia, north-east of the Viking 1 landing site and much closer to the northern polar region.

The consecutive landing of two operating spacecraft on Mars is a spectacular milestone in planetary exploration. The Viking mission, eight years in the making, has cost 1,000 million dollars and involved the work of 10,000 people at various times.

The aim of America's costly Viking project is to discover if there is, or has been, life on Mars. Scientists recognize the hazards of conducting by computer biological experiments more than 200 million miles away.

First reports to mission control at Pasadena, California reported surprisingly large amounts of oxygen in the Martian soil and the formation of carbon dioxide by something – animate or inanimate – in the soil. The first photograph showed rocks with a porous structure. Colour pictures show red soil and pink sky.

The Pioneer-10 space probe (launched from Cape Kennedy on February 28th, 1972) passed through most of the asteroid belt between Jupiter and Mars – a region never before penetrated by any man-made object.

The Russians, too, have launched unmanned spacecraft towards Mars to carry out scientific research around the planet.

A joint enterprise, labelled the Apollo-Soyuz test project, was agreed in May 1972 between the United States and the Soviet Union for a common docking system for future generations of craft: a universal rescue system for use should one or the other of their craft become marooned in space.

On July 15th, 1975, Apollo was launched from Cape Canaveral, Florida, $7\frac{1}{2}$ hours after Russia's Soyuz lifted off from Baikonur, Soviet Kazakhstan – the first time two vehicles had been built for launching deliberately on the same day for a collaborative venture. They orbited separately in the same direction around earth before docking over Germany on 17th July. The five astronauts tested the docking system developed over the previous three years and used it to exchange visits between the two craft.

On November 19th, 1975, an unmanned Soviet spaceship docked with the orbiting space laboratory, Salyut 4, for the first time. The docking was automatic, controlled by two computers on board the two craft.

Man's Exploration of Space

Date 1961	Pilot	Country	Spacecraft	Flight Duration days hrs. min.		
April 12th	Yuri Gagarin (27) (First man in space)	USSR	Vostok 1	1	48	
May 5th	Alan B. Shepard (37) (First American in space)	USA	Freedom 7		15	
July 21st	Virgil Grissom (34)	USA	Liberty Bell 7		16	

Aug. 6th–7th	Gherman Stepanovich Titov (26)	USSR	Vostok 2	1	1	18
1962						
Feb. 20th	John Glenn (40) (First American manned spacecraft to enter Earth orbit)	USA	Friendship		4	55
May 24th	Malcolm Scott Carpenter (37)	USA	Aurora 7		4	56
Aug. 11th–15th	Andrian Grigoryevich Nikolayev (32) (First man-operated television from space)	USSR	Vostok 3	3	22	22
Aug. 12th–15th	Pavel Romanovich Popovich (31)	USSR	Vostok 4	2	22	57
Oct. 3rd	Walter Marty Schirra (39)	USA	Sigma 7		9	13
1963						
May 15th–16th	Leroy Gordon Cooper (36) (Manual re-entry after failure of automatic control system)	USA	Faith 7	1	10	20
June 14th–19th	Valeriy Fyodorovich Bykovsky (28)	USSR	Vostok 5	4	23	66
June 16th–19th	Valentina Vladimirovna Tereshkova (26) (First woman in space)	USSR	Vostok 6	3	22	50
1964						
Oct. 12th–13th	Vladimir Mihailovich Komarov (37); Boris Borisovich Yegorov (37); Konstantin Petrovich Feoktiskov (38)	USSR	Voskhod 1	1	0	17
1965						
March 18th–19th	Aleksey Arkhipovich Leonov (30); Pavel Ivanovich Belyavev (39) (Leonov became first man to float in outer space)	USSR	Voskhod 2	1	2	2
March 23rd	Virgil Ivan Grissom (38); John Watts Young	USA	Gemini 3		4	53

June 3rd–7th	James McDivitt (35); Edward Higgins White (34) (White took first space walk by an American)	USA	Gemini 4	4	1	56
Aug. 21st–29th	Leroy Gordon Cooper (38); Charles Conrad (35)	USA	Gemini 5	7	22	56
Dec. 4th–18th	Frank Borman (37); James Lovell (37); (rendezvous with Gemini 6)	USA	Gemini 7	13	18	35
Dec. 15th–16th	Walter Marty Schirra (43); Thomas P. Stafford (35)	USA	Gemini 6	1	1	51
1966						
March 16th	Neil Alden Armstrong (36); David Randolph Scott (36); (First docking between manned and unmanned spacecraft – Agena 7)	USA	Gemini 8		10	42
June 3rd–6th	Thomas P. Stafford (36) Eugene Andrew Cernan (32) (Longest space walk to date – 129 minutes by Cernan)	USA	Gemini 9	3	0	21
July 18th–21st	John Watts Young; Michael Collins (space walk by Collins)	USA	Gemini 10	2	23	14
Sept. 12th–15th	Charles Conrad (36); Richard F. Gordon (space walk by Gordon)	USA	Gemini 11	2	23	17
Nov. 11th–15th	James A. Lovell (38); Edwin Eugene Aldrin (36); (Docking with an Agena vehicle. Space walks by Aldrin totalling 5½ hours)	USA	Gemini 12	3	22	35
1967						
April 22nd–23rd	Vladimir Mikhailovich Komarov (40) (Killed when his landing parachute tangled)	USSR	Soyuz 1	1	2	45
Oct. 11th–22nd	Walter Marty Schirra (45); Donn F. Eisele (38); R. Walter Cunningham (36) (First flight of capsule designed ultimately for 7-day voyage to the Moon)	USA	Apollo VII	10	20	9

Oct. 26th–30th(47)	Georgiy T. Beregovoiy (Rendezvous with unmanned Soyuz 2)	USSR	Soyuz 3	3	22	51
Dec. 21st–27th	Frank Borman (40); James Lovell (40); William A. Anders (35) (First men to break free from the Earth's gravitational field. First men to orbit the Moon. Christmas radio greetings sent from astronauts while in Moon orbit)	USA	Apollo VIII	6	3	0

1969

Jan. 14th–17th	Vladimir Shatalov (41); Alexei Yeliseyev (34); Yevgeny Khrunov (35)	USSR	Soyuz 4	3	23	14
Jan. 15th–18th	Boris Volynov (34); (Docked with Soyuz 4. First joining of two manned spacecraft in orbit. Yeliseyev and Khrunov transferred to – and landed in – Soyuz 5)	USSR	Soyuz 5	3	0	46
March 3rd–13th	James McDivitt (39); David Randolph Scott (36); Russell Louis Schweikart (33) (First trial of module – manned – in space. Crew transferred through interior connexion)	USA	Apollo IX	10	1	1
May 18th–26th	Thomas P. Stafford (38); John Watts Young (38); Eugene Andrew Cernan (35)	USA	Apollo X	8	0	3
July 16th–24th	Neil Alden Armstrong (38); Edwin Eugene Aldrin (39); Michael Collins (First Moon landing by man – Armstrong. Moon rock brought back to Earth)	USA	Apollo XI	8	3	18

Oct. 11th–16th	Giorgiy Shonin (34); Valery N. Kubasov (34);	USSR	Soyuz 6	4	22	42
Oct. 12th–17th	Anatoly V. Filipchenko (41); Viktor V. Gorbatko (35); Vladislav N. Volkov (34)	USSR	Soyuz 7	4	22	41
Oct. 13th–18th	Vladimir A. Shatalov (41); Alexei N. Yeliseyev (35) (Rendezvous and formation trials and experiments)	USSR	Soyuz 8	4	22	41
Nov. 14th–24th	Charles Conrad (39); Richard F. Gordon (40); Alan L. Bean (37) (Second Moon landing by man – Conrad. Moon soil brought back to Earth)	USA	Apollo XII	10	4	36

1970

April 11th	James Lovell (42); Fred Haise (36); John Swigert (38) (Landing on Moon abandoned after explosion in service module of spacecraft)	USA	Apollo XIII	5	22	54
June 1st	Andrian Nikolayev (33); Vitaly Sevastoyanov (35)	USSR	Soyuz 9	17	17	0

1971

Jan. 31st	Alan Shepard (47); Edgar Mitchell (40); Stuart Roosa (37)	USA	Apollo XIV	9	0	2
April 23rd	Vladimir Shatalov (43); Alexei Yeliseyev (36); Nikolai Rukavishnikov (39)	USSR	Soyuz 10	1	23	45
June 6th	Georgy Dobrovolsky (43); Vladislav Volkov (35); Viktor Patsayev (37) (Spent 24 days in space but when spacecraft returned to Earth the three cosmonauts were found dead in their seats)	USSR	Soyuz 11			

Date	Crew	Country	Mission			
July 26th	David Scott (39); Alfred Worden (39); James Irwin (41)	USA	Apollo XV	12	7	12
1972 April 16th	John W. Young (41); Charles M. Duke (36); Thomas K. Mattingly (36)	USA	Apollo XVI	11	1	51
Dec. 7th	Harrison Schmitt (37) Eugene Cernan (39) Ronald Evans (Collected red and orange rock: left complex package of instruments on Moon which continue to send back messages)	USA	Apollo XVII	12	16	32
1973 Sept. 27th	Vasili Lazarev (45); Oleg Makarov (40)	USSR	Soyuz 12	2		
Dec. 18th	Pyotr Killimuk (31); Valentin Lebedev (31)	USSR	Soyuz 13	8		
1974 June 25th			Salyut 3			
July 3rd	Pavel Popovich (44); Zyuri Artyukhin (44) (to link with above)	USSR	Soyuz 14	16		
Aug. 27th	Gennady Sarafanov (32); Lev Demin (48)	USSR	Soyuz 15	2		
Dec. 2nd	Anatoly Filipchenko (47); Nikolai Rukavishnikov (41) (In preparation for American Soviet docking experiment scheduled for July 1975)	USSR	Soyuz 16			
Dec.		USSR	Salyut 4			
1975 Jan. 11th	Alexei Gubarev (43); Georgy Grecho (43) (To link with Salyut 4 – a further stage in the development of orbital laboratories)	USSR	Soyuz 17	29	13	20

May 25th– July 26th	Col. Pyotr Klimuk & Vitali Sevastianov (Soviet record for space endurance)	USSR	Salyut 4	63 days on board orbiting space station
June 22nd		USSR	Salyut 5	
July 6th	Col. Boris Volynov (41); Vitaly Zholobov (39) (to carry out joint experiments with orbital space laboratory Salyut 5)	USSR	Soyuz 21	
July 15th–	Col. Alexei Leonov & Valeri Kubasov	USSR	Soyuz	⎫
July 24th	Brigadier-Gen. Thomas Stafford, Vance Brand & Donald Slayton (51) (First Soviet–American link-up in space. First time TV cameras showed scene inside Apollo Command Module during lift-off; first time a Soviet landing televised live from helicopters)	USA	Apollo	⎬ Salyut 4 ⎭

12 SPORT

Angling

Among the most ancient of human activities is that of catching fish by means of a baited hook or 'angle'. The taking of fish for sport is a modern idea. The two branches of the sport – angling in fresh water and fishing in the sea – have much in common.

Archery

One of the oldest arts still being practised today.

Archers are called 'toxophilites', a word which comes from the Greek *toxon* meaning bow. The shooting of arrows with a bow dates back to at least 30,000 and, more probably, nearer 50,000 years ago. The stout English longbow, made of yew, and with a cloth-yard shaft, won victory for the English at famous battles at Crecy, Agincourt and Poitiers. American Indians used the bow for hunting and fishing; pygmy tribes of Africa used poison on their arrows.

Many British monarchs practised archery. Henry VIII 'shotte as stronge and as greate a lengthe as anie of his garde'. George IV, as Prince of Wales, became patron in 1787 of the Royal Toxophilite society, although the Royal Company of Archers of Edinburgh is older by more than a century.

Badminton

Was first played in India by the English military in the early 1870s. They called it Poona.

Badminton is a court or lawn game played with lightweight rackets and shuttlecocks and consists entirely of volleying – *i.e.* the shuttle must be struck in mid-air before it touches the floor or ground. It may be derived from another game called battledore and shuttlecock, a game almost identical with a game represented in ancient Greek drawings and which has been popular in China, Japan, India and Siam for at least 2,000 years. The name was given to the game by some English army officers home on leave from India in 1873 who played it at Badminton, the country estate of the Duke of Beaufort in Gloucestershire.

Ballooning

Balloons did not result, as did aeroplanes, from man's ability to adapt nature's methods to his own use. They resulted from his own creative genius. In 1783, the Montgolfier brothers, Jacques Etienne and Joseph, filled a bag with smoke from a straw fire and watched it rise. One of the early long-distance balloon flights was that of Wise who flew 800 miles from St Louis, Missouri to Henderson, New York in 1859.

Interest in ballooning as a sport was increased when James Gordon Bennett offered a trophy and a money prize to the winner of an annual long-distance race. It was won three years in succession (1922–24) by Belgium, but the races were not revived after the Second World War.

Races have often been run to see who, starting at a certain place, could land nearest to a particular spot. The widespread increase in electric-power lines has increased the dangers of landing.

Basketball

Invented in 1891 by James Naismith (1861–1939), a Canadian, a graduate of McGill university and Presbyterian Theological College, who became a student – later an instructor – in physical education at the International YMCA training school at Springfield, Mass.

Naismith was asked by the head of the physical education department at Springfield to devise an indoor game for the students – a game not dissimilar to football or baseball. And so was invented the only major sport of strictly US origin. The popularity of basketball gradually spread and its acceptance by Yale in 1894 induced other institutions to play the game. It was played in Canada in 1892, and introduced in France the following year by Mel Rideout who also demonstrated it in London on the 50th anniversary of the founding of the YMCA in June 1894.

Billiards

Nothing is known about the origin of billiards. It may be inferred only that it developed from a variety of games in which propelling a ball was the main feature. The various games of billiards include pocket billiards (pool), snooker, carom (or cannon), and English billiards. The game became fashionable during the reign of King Louis XIV who was advised to play it every day after dinner. In its modern form it dates back to about 1800. Billiards is played by both amateurs and professionals and the sole governing body for the sport is the Billiards Association and Control Council.

Bobsledding

Originated in Switzerland around 1890. Runners were added to toboggans to increase speed when sliding down ice-covered natural or artificial slopes. Early bobsleds were built mostly of wood but steel runners were soon adopted.

The sport grew in popularity and in 1898 the first organized competition was held on the Cresta run at St Moritz. Bobsledding became an internationally recognized sport and was included in the first Winter Olympic games at Chamonix, France, in 1924.

Bowling

The history of bowling can be traced back 7,000 years. Stone-age men and boys played some sort of bowling game in which large rocks and pebbles were rolled at pointed stones or sheep joints. Early Polynesians participated in an ancient game of bowling, one rule of which was that the stones were to be bowled a distance of 60 ft – the same specification used in tenpin bowling today.

Bowls

One of the oldest of outdoor pastimes. The game is different from bowling in that the aim is to roll the bowls near a stationary ball called a jack. But there are certain points of similarity and both are of very ancient origin.

The game of bowls was certainly played in the 13th century, and the amount of skill needed was increased considerably in the 16th century when biased bowls were introduced. Women were accustomed to playing bowls in Shakespeare's time and Sir Francis Drake finished his game of bowls on Plymouth Hoe before tackling the Spaniards beating up the Channel.

Boxing

Boxing existed in ancient Crete, where a civilization was established by about 1500 BC. It was a sport practised by the ancient Greeks, who believed in the development of physical as well as mental abilities. They called it 'pugilism' or fist fighting. Fighters wore soft leather thongs bound about their fists and often up their forearms to protect hands and wrists. Later, harder leather was used for the thongs with the result that they became weapons and, late in the history of the Roman Empire, the hand covering was studded with iron or brass nuggets and was used in battles to the death in Roman arenas. Boxing was introduced into the Olympic Games in 688 BC.

Pugilism evidently ceased with the rise of Christianity and the fall of the Roman empire. The bare-knuckle era began with the rise of London as a major city. Prize-fighters performed for agreed purses. There were few rules until Jack Broughton, a 200-pound Englishman, who won the championship of his country sometime between 1734 and 1740, won a new respect for prize-fighting, fighting by a set of rules which governed boxing, with only minor changes, until 1838 when they were superseded by the

London Prize Ring rules. Then John Graham Chambers devised a new set of rules to which John Sholto Douglas, 8th Marquess of Queensberry, lent his name, to emphasize the science and skill of boxing, and the Queensberry rules gained favour steadily.

Modern boxing is the art of attack and defence. The contestants wear padded gloves, fight bouts of 3 minutes, do not wrestle, and otherwise observe the code set out in the Marquess of Queensberry rules. Styles of boxing have undergone great changes but with the increase in popularity of the sport as a spectacle, crowds frequently demand a knock-out or, at least, plenty of action. Boxing in seven divisions was introduced into the modern Olympic Games in 1904, all the titles being won by United States boxers.

Canoeing

The sport of canoeing dates from 1865 when the canoe *Rob Roy* was designed by John MacGregor for long journeys by water and yet was light enough to be carried overland. Weighing about 70 pounds, it could be propelled by both double-bladed paddle and sails. In Canada, team racing with single-bladed paddles in 'war canoes' is a popular amateur sport.

Cricket

Cricket has been played under recognized rules at least since the beginning of the 18th century: a written code appeared in 1744. An early written reference to the game appears in Edward I's reign and cricket was being played by schoolboys in Guildford about 1550. Oliver Cromwell played cricket and football; in 1654 seven parishioners of Eltham were fined for playing cricket on a Sunday.

It was in Sussex in 1697 that the first definite match of which there is a record was played. There were eleven players a side – and a stake of 50 guineas. In 1719 'the Londoners' met 'the Kentish men' in what was virtually the first County match.

Early cricket bats were no doubt the shaped branches of trees; the ball was probably much the same in the 17th century as it is today – it was stuffed with hair or hemp, dyed crimson and leather-covered; the 'regulation' wicket, according to an important authority in 1706, was 22 inches ✕

6 inches, the popping crease (or 'scratch' – whitening did not come in until the famous W. G. Grace's time) was 46 inches in front of it and the pitch was 22 yards long. All these measurements correspond with divisions or multiples of the early Tudor units of length measure.

An important stage in the development of cricket was the rise of the Hambledon club – a little Hampshire village known as 'the cradle of cricket'. For 30 years they challenged and held at bay all comers, even beating a representative England XI by an innings and 168 runs.

Lord's, the acknowledged Mecca of all cricketers, was first opened as a private ground by Thomas Lord, a Yorkshireman. The Marylebone Cricket Club (the MCC), with its home at Lord's, was founded in 1788 and was accepted throughout the world as the authoritative source of all cricket legislation. In 1836 the first North v South match was played – clear evidence of the way cricket had spread throughout the country.

A match between women's teams is first recorded in 1747 and the game continued to be played by women throughout the 19th century. A series of exhibition matches between two regular elevens trained by professional coaches was held in 1890 but the modern development of women's cricket is marked by the formation of the English Women's Cricket association in 1927. Women played cricket for the first time at Lord's on August 4th, 1976.

Croquet

A game popular among the royal families of France in the 17th century. By 1850 it was one of the most popular outdoor sports in England and had become the game of kings and queens. Croquet evolved, it is said, from the *paille-maille* which was played in the 13th century. The All-England Croquet club was formed in 1870, the annual contest for the championship taking place at Wimbledon. After ten years or so croquet, a popular game at garden parties, was practically ousted by lawn tennis but, with improved implements and a more scientific form of play, was revived in the late 1890s.

The United All England Croquet association was formed in 1896–7. There are several versions of croquet and the rules and court dimensions differ. Tactics play an important part in the game.

Falconry

A favourite sport of the aristocracy in the middle ages. Often called hawking. Known in China some 2000 years BC and in Japan, India, Arabia, Iran and Syria around 600 BC.

Falconry was probably introduced into England from the Continent about AD 860 where it was a very popular sport until about the middle of the 17th century. The enclosure of waste lands and the introduction of firearms contributed to its loss of popularity. However, interest revived slightly after World War II.

Hawks are trained mainly through the appetite, but patience, gentleness and care are required to fit them for use.

Fencing

Modern fencing is practised with three different weapons – the foil, épée (or duelling sword) and sabre. It is a worldwide sport, the objective being to score by touching the opponent's target and to avoid being touched. Fencing has been a major Olympic sport since the games were revived in 1896. Its ruling body, the Fédération Internationale d'Escrime (FIE), was founded in 1913. Fencing can be enjoyed by a wide age group and by both men and women.

Fencing as a pure sport dates from roughly the 18th century, although the fencing bout in *Hamlet* indicates that friendly tests of skill in swordsmanship were well established by 1600.

The rules of fencing were based on certain conventions of play originally adopted for safety reasons before the mask was introduced – e.g. the target was then limited to the trunk of the body.

Sabre fencing dates from the middle of the 19th century. The conventions of foil play were adapted to a light practice weapon introduced by the Italians and a new dimension was added to the diversity and complexity of the actions when scoring could be done by both the point and cutting edge.

Épée fencing began late in the 19th century as a reaction to the conventions of foil play. Épée fencing is the most popular form of sport in international competition, and is one of the sports in the modern pentathlon.

Football

Modern games grouped under the general heading of 'football' developed in ancient Britain out of the mêlées in which a round or oval object was kicked, punched, or carried to some goal. The mêlées may well have arisen from the apparently instinctive desire of a child to kick any object in its path.

The Romans played a game called *harpastum* ('handball'). Medieval mêlées always seemed to take place on Shrove Tuesday, a day of festival before a fast, but as their popularity increased matches were played on village greens at all times. The sport became so popular that Kings of England feared it would distract the youth of the country from the study of archery and that the efficiency of armies would suffer. Edward III decided to ban football for military reasons, as did Richard II, Henry IV, Henry VIII and Elizabeth I – but these edicts were not effective in the long run. Violence seems to have been a feature of the game in the 18th century and broken shins and broken heads were among the minor casualties.

Football became more of a regular pastime with the growth of the English public schools where boys did not enjoy their sports individually. They adopted the team games previously played by the working man. There was at this time no governing body for the game and the only rule universally applied seems to have been that the ball must never be carried or passed by hand in the direction of the opponent's goal.

This rule was broken at Rugby School in 1823 when, a commemorative stone records, 'William Webb Ellis with a fine disregard for the rules of football as played in his time, first took the ball in his arms and ran with it, thus originating the distinctive feature of the Rugby game'.

It was impossible to play matches against other schools as each school had its own rules for the game. Eventually, a number of independent clubs came into being and soon both soccer and 'rugger' had rules and governing bodies.

The industrial revolution, and the consequent collection of people in the towns led to the sport spreading, until association football was known the world over and rugby was a popular sport in the Commonwealth, in France and elsewhere.

The Football Association is the ruling body of the game in England. It was formed in 1863. Professionalism entered the game around 1881, and was legalized in 1885. The Football Association organized the first of a series of knockout competitions for the FA Cup in 1871–72 which soon became world famous. Immediately after the coming of professionalism attendances at Cup Ties began to increase rapidly. Later, the Association put up another trophy for competition among amateur clubs.

In 1888 William McGregor, known as 'father of the League', suggested to professional clubs that they should combine and form a league, arranging a championship on the basis of home-and-away matches with each other. Twelve clubs formed the original Football League for the 1888–89 season. The Football League Cup was introduced in 1960. Football pools were organized depending on the Football league results.

Once association football had become popular in Great Britain it was only a matter of time before it spread throughout the world. Other countries started their own clubs and a world tournament was organized in 1930 by the Fédération Internationale de Football Association (FIFA), for the Jules Rimet Cup, commonly known as the World Cup. This tournament is an open one in which amateurs and professionals compete on level terms. World championships are held every four years.

The European Cup was inaugurated in 1955. Each season the champion club of each Association in the European Union of Football Associations is eligible to compete with the winner of the previous season's competition.

Immediately after the forming of the Rugby Union in 1871 the game spread rapidly abroad. Rugby League, played mainly in the north of England, Australia, New Zealand and France, is a direct descendant of Rugby Union.

As a result of an argument about whether players should be compensated for loss of earnings sustained as a result of playing the game, twenty-two clubs from Yorkshire, Lancashire and Cheshire left the Rugby Union in 1895 and founded what became known as the Rugby League. The major differences between Rugby League and Rugby Union today are that Rugby League is played on a professional or an amateur basis with thirteen players and Rugby Union is played on an amateur basis with fifteen players.

The Rugby League Challenge Cup competition was inaugurated in 1897, the winners being Batley who defeated St Helens.

Gliding

Man-made gliders have no engines and are heavier than air. Gliders soar, using upward motions of the air or pulsations in the wind, thus enabling man to fly long distances, to reach high altitudes and remain aloft for days.

Otto Lilienthal began to make experiments in 1867, having accumulated much information from a study of the flight of birds. He built a man-carrying glider with a framework of peeled willow rods covered with tough cotton fabric. The great American exponents of gliding were the Wright Brothers.

An increased knowledge of meteorology gave rise to different ways of soaring, of which the two most important are thermal soaring and thunder-storm flight. Modern soaring planes can be put through most of the manoeuvres practised by pilots of powered planes.

Gliders have been used in war and have been flown with as many as 130 men aboard. They are used for meteorological and aeronautical research as well as for sport.

Golf

The game of golf as we know it today originated in Scotland, but it is not known when or where. The first written reference to golf appeared in 1457 when the Parliament of King James II of Scotland decreed that 'fute-ball and golfe be utterly cryed downe, and not to be used', because they inter-fered with the practice of archery, essential for the defence of the country. Two subsequent parliaments issued similar decrees – but none was success-ful.

Het kolven, a game played in the Netherlands, provides some of the terminology of the game. The word golf comes from the Dutch *kolf* which is related to the German *Kolbe* and the Danish *holbe*, meaning 'club'. The mound on which a Dutchman placed his ball was a *tuitje*, pronounced 'toytee' and the hole he aimed at was a *put*.

The Royal Blackheath Golf club of London is thought to be the oldest existing golf club in the world. The earliest known rules are the thirteen recorded in the first minute book of the Honourable Company of Edin-burgh Golfers.

The Royal and Ancient Golf Club of St Andrews, Scotland, formed in 1754, became the governing body for men's golf in the British Isles and throughout most of the Commonwealth. A Ladies' Golf Club was formed at St Andrews in 1872, and the Ladies' Golf Union, which governs women's golf, was organized in 1893.

There are two distinct forms of play: match play and stroke (medal) play. In the former the player and his opponent play together and compete only against each other, while in the latter each player competes against every other player in the tournament.

Gymnastics

Gymnastics are practised either as a sport or to promote physical development. The history of gymnastics dates back to ancient Greece but the revival of interest in all sports in the 19th century brought with it the modern development of gymnastics.

Gymnastics was one of the first sports to recognize that its therapeutic advantages are as valuable to men as to women, requiring a high level of discipline of both mind and body.

Hockey

Also called field-hockey to distinguish it from ice hockey (qv).

The ancient Persians played a crude form of a game with sticks and there is evidence to show that probably most of the Indian tribes in America played a rough stick game for several thousand years. Traces of such a game as played by the Aztec Indians have been found in America. A game resembling modern hockey began to be played in England about 1875.

The Hockey Association (later to be called the International Hockey board), formed in 1886, marked the beginning of modern hockey and in 1895 the first international match was played, England beating Ireland by five goals to nil.

Hockey is played extensively in many countries by women.

Horse Racing

Horses had been used for riding more than a thousand years before the first historical record of races for mounted horses is given in connection with the XXXIII Olympiad, about 624 BC.

Contests of speed between horses are among the oldest pastimes of man. A text on the breeding and training of horses, written about 1500 BC, was found in Asia Minor. The earliest full-length account of a chariot race appears in the *Iliad*.

Modern organized racing began in the British Isles where it is known as 'the sport of kings'. The first mention of a formal event for a money prize was in the reign of Richard I when £40 in 'ready gold' was competed for by knights over a 3-mile course. The earliest mention of an established race meeting is of that held at Chester.

The rise in popularity of the turf dates from James I, who had previously patronized the sport in Scotland. Charles II was known as 'father of the British turf', and it was his patronage that brought Newmarket to its position as the headquarters of racing and breeding. The patronage of Queen Anne gave Ascot its distinction. The St Leger at Doncaster, Yorkshire, was the first-established of what are now known as the Classics.

Hurdling

The first hurdling races were held at Eton College about 1837. The competitors ran and jumped over each hurdle in turn, landing on both feet, thus checking their momentum. But in 1840, a new form of hurdling came into use and hurdlers began to 'sail' over the hurdles with the body upright, the front leg curled under the body and the rear leg trailing. Standard numbers of steps between hurdles were introduced and further refinements were made about 1885 when a straight front leg with a forward lunge of the body was shown to provide a better clearance. This 'step-over' action is the basis of the modern hurdling style.

Hurling

Hurling is the national pastime of Ireland and there are many references to it in old Irish manuscripts.

It is a game played with stick and ball, outdoors, and is rather like hockey (qv). The stick is called a hurley.

It was, for a long time, played between rival parishes with an unlimited number of players on either side, and games were often played for money.

Ice-Hockey

Ice-hockey is thought to be either a development of field hockey or a development of the old Irish game of hurling. There is evidence that the Indians played such a game in Canada centuries ago.

Canada established the sport and was the first country to organize the game on a nationwide basis. For many years it was played on natural ice, but with the building of ice-rinks (indoor and outdoor) its popularity spread rapidly.

The disc-like object with which the game is played is called a puck.

Ice Skating

Dates back at least to the 8th century. The earliest known skate is the bone runner. Cow bones (or sometimes bones of sheep, reindeer or other large animals) were ground down and shaped to a flat surface and bound to the feet with thongs. The modern Dutch word *schaats*, from which is derived the English word 'skates', is at least as old as 1573. The early history of skating can be traced in literature. Samuel Pepys and John Evelyn both wrote in their diaries of watching ice skaters in St James's Park on December 1st, 1662. Skating is widely recorded in art: one of the earliest known pictures of skating is a woodcut dated 1448 illustrating an accident which befell St Lidwina, patron saint of skaters, in 1396.

Ice-skating became a major sport with the invention of refrigeration and the introduction of ice-rinks. Ice-shows, professional skating spectaculars, were established as a popular form of entertainment by the second half of the 20th century.

Figure skating requires skill in plain skating, a high degree of body control and a great deal of practice. The American, Jackson Haines, known as 'the father of figure skating', influenced modern figure skating and combined dance movements with skating. The oldest skating club in the world is the Edinburgh Skating club, founded in 1642.

Ju-Jitsu (Judo)

Originally known as Japanese wrestling, it is a method of self-defence and offence without weapons in personal encounter. For centuries it was taught secretly as an art in Japan, but eventually became a popular sport and is taught in schools and gymnasiums as well as to army, navy and police recruits.

There are many varieties of ju-jitsu: Jigoro Kano founded the most popular style in 1882 and called it judo.

The progress made by students is indicated by a belt colour: novices wear white belts and more experienced students a brown belt. Only rarely do exponents of the sport reach the degree of expertise which entitles them to wear the coveted black belt.

Karting

Karting is a form of motor racing. It is cheap and exciting.

Karts and karting are American inventions and it is a modern sport which began only in 1956. The following year the first meeting of the Go Kart Club of America was convened.

The sport developed quickly in Britain and a demonstration was given at a Silverstone motor race meeting after which the RAC drew up some rules for karting upon which international regulations were subsequently based.

Other karting activities include springing, hill-climbing and dragging. Karting is now a popular sport in Europe, the USA, Australia and New Zealand, Japan and the USSR.

Lawn Tennis

The game of lawn tennis had its beginning in England, and was invented by an Englishman, Major Walter Wingfield. In 1874 he devised and patented a 'new and improved portable court for playing the ancient game of tennis'.

The first championship was held on grass courts at Wimbledon in 1877. There were twenty-two competitors. From 1877–1907 the championships at Wimbledon were won by natives of the British Isles. But those early tournaments bore little resemblance to their successors.

Lawn tennis quickly spread to other continents. It was played by men and women from the start, but women did not compete in competitive tournaments until 1884, when Maud Watson became the first women's champion at Wimbledon.

In those days the game was played chiefly from the base line. Women served underhand. The game of lawn tennis is played not only on grass, but on dirt, clay, concrete, wood and on courts made of a composition.

The oldest and most outstanding individual lawn tennis tournament of the world is Wimbledon. The Wimbledon Championships have always been played on grass. Professionals first played there in 1968.

The outstanding team event is the contest for the Davis Cup, which began as a challenge match between Great Britain and the United States in 1900. The Davis Cup, more properly called the International Lawn Tennis Championship, is competed for on a knock-out principle and is divided into three zones – the European, American and Eastern.

The Wightman Cup, for competition between teams of women players from the United States and England, was donated in 1923. It is competed for annually, the contest being held alternately in the two countries. It is officially called the Ladies' International Lawn Tennis Championship.

Olympic Games

The origin of the Olympic Games is not known exactly but there is a historical record of the ancient games beginning in 776 BC. They were held at four-yearly intervals until AD 394 when they were abolished after Greece lost its independence.

At first the programme was confined to one day and there was only one race. Then the games were extended to seven days and additional races were added as well as the discus and javelin throw, boxing, wrestling, chariot races, the pentathlon and many other events. The games were restricted to Greeks. Women were not allowed to compete nor to watch. Prior to the contest all competitors and their families, judges and trainers swore a solemn oath to keep the competition clean and fair and to give just decisions.

Nowadays the Olympic Oath is pronounced on behalf of all the assembled athletes by a contestant from the country where the Games are taking place. It runs: 'In the name of all competitors I promise that we will take part in these Olympic Games, respecting and abiding by the rules which govern them, in the true spirit of sportsmanship, for the glory of sport and for the honour of our teams.'

The games were so important in the life of Greece that time was measured by the four-year interval between them – an Olympiad. The greatest honour then – competed for by kings and commoners – was the simple branch of wild olive given to a victor in the games.

The modern Olympic games were revived by Baron Pierre de Coubertin and were held under the royal patronage of the King of Greece in Athens in 1896. A new marble stadium was purpose-built. Meetings have been scheduled as follows:

Athens	1896	Berlin	1936
Paris	1900	Tokyo, then	
St Louis	1904	Helsinki	1940**
Athens	1906*	London	1944**
London	1908	London	1948
Stockholm	1912	Helsinki	1952
Berlin	1916**	Melbourne	1956***
Antwerp	1920	Rome	1960
Paris	1924	Tokyo	1964
Amsterdam	1928	Mexico	1968
Los Angeles	1932	Munich	1972
		Montreal	1976

*intercalated celebration or unofficial Games
**cancelled due to World Wars
***equestrian events held at Stockholm, Sweden

Separate winter games were begun in 1924 at Chamonix, France.

Contestants in the Olympic games must be amateurs. The Olympic Village, where special housing is provided for all competitors, was first featured in Los Angeles at the 1932 games. The sacred Olympic flame, which burns in the Olympic stadium throughout the games, is ignited by a torch from Olympia, the site of the original games in Greece, and carried to the stadium by relays of runners. For the 1976 Games it was transmitted to Montreal by satellite.

Each Olympiad sees records broken in almost every sport. The pro- gramme usually includes athletics (track and field), gymnastics, boxing, fencing, shooting, wrestling, rowing, swimming, equestrianism, modern pentathlon, cycling, weight-lifting, yachting and optional events such as soccer, water polo, field hockey, basketball and canoeing. Winter games normally include skiing, skating, ice hockey and bobsled. There is no maximum or minimum age limit.

Orienteering

Competitors navigate across country between control points. Maps and compasses are used. Orienteering develops athletic and academic skills and runners enjoy both physical and mental exercise. It is a popular personal sport and is used as a training activity in some schools.

Orienteering was first introduced in Sweden in 1918 and spread rapidly from Scandinavia across to East and West Europe. World championship matches are held bi-annually.

Polo

The earliest records of polo are Persian. The word polo comes from the Tibetan *pulu*, 'a ball'.

The first European polo club was formed in 1859, the Calcutta polo club the following year and, in 1869, the 10th Hussars, after reading an account of the game in India, started to play polo in England. The first recorded match took place on Hounslow Heath in 1871 between the 9th Lancers and the 10th Hussars, with eight players a side.

The first rules were drawn up with the founding of the Hurlingham Polo Club in 1874. Polo is now played with four players on each side, on exactly the same principles as hockey or association football. A match lasts about an hour and is divided into periods of play called chukkers. Ponies are changed during the intervals between the periods of play.

The cost of the game increased considerably after the First World War. Ponies were difficult to obtain and after World War II it looked as if the sport was finished. But Viscount Cowdray began a revival with the Cowdray Park Polo Club. Other old clubs revived and new ones started. A Coronation tournament was organized in 1953, and now large crowds of spectators attend polo matches.

Rowing

In ancient times rowing was the chief means of propelling war vessels: nowadays, it is confined almost entirely to small boats.

The Thames is considered the cradle of rowing as a pastime and as a competitive sport in modern times. Nobility and gentry who had fine mansions on the banks of the River Thames relied almost entirely on their fitted barges as a means of conveyance. In 1454 a Lord Mayor of London 'built a noble barge and was rowed by watermen with silver oars'. In the 16th and 17th centuries competitions took place between the watermen of which the race for the 'Doggett's Coat and Badge' still survives today.

The first English regatta took place on the Thames in 1775.

The first race between Oxford and Cambridge was rowed in 1829 over a 2-mile course at Henley, as the result of a challenge issued to Oxford 'that the University of Cambridge hereby challenge the University of Oxford to row a match at or near London each in an eight-oared boat during the Easter vacation'. In 1845 it was rowed from Putney to Mortlake, a distance of 4 miles 374 yards, and it is now an annual event which attracts huge crowds.

The Henley Royal Regatta, established in 1839, brings together the best of English crews and, in the open events, attracts competitors from Europe, Australia, America and elsewhere.

Steeplechasing and Hurdle Racing

This form of racing can be traced back directly to the chase and the field of battle, where horses of great size, speed and agility were required. Cavalry officers and sportsmen enjoyed the excitement and danger of the hunt.

Administration is in the hands of the National Hunt committee and many of the most important fixed events are run at various hunt club meetings over difficult cross-country courses.

The Grand National, a handicap steeplechase, was first run over the Aintree course at Liverpool in 1839. It attracts world-wide enthusiasm and interest, as does the Derby. The course is dangerous and difficult – but the prestige and material rewards that go with victory are great.

Swimming

A sport and a pastime enjoyed by millions. Also a means of protecting and saving lives.

The ability to swim was practised widely in many ancient civilizations including Egypt, Assyria, Greece and Rome. During the Middle Ages, swimming was not popular because of the belief that it helped to spread epidemics.

Swimming was one of the sports included in the first modern Olympic Games at Athens in 1896. Diving events were added in 1904 and women's swimming and diving in 1912.

Tennis

Tennis was a popular game with various kings of England and France. The origin of the game is obscure, but may be derived from the word *Tenez!* (Take it! Play!). A lot of French words are used in the game, *e.g. grille, tambout, dedans.*

Henry II is described as the best player in France. Later Henry IV and Louis XIV were patrons and players of tennis. There was a court at Windsor Castle in the time of Henry VII. Henry VIII built a court at Hampton Court Palace in 1529–30 which is still in use today. Pepys frequently refers to tennis and there is a mention of the game in Shakespeare's *Henry V.*

The game, which is played in a walled and roofed court, was at the peak of its popularity in the 16th and 17th centuries, but it lost some of its popularity in the 19th century, mainly because many of the courts were demolished for rebuilding programmes. (*See also* Lawn Tennis).

Tobogganing

The sport of sliding down snow-covered slopes and artificial ice-covered chutes on a runnerless sled.

The toboggan was originally a primitive sled used by American Indians and made of poles tied together. Tobogganing as a sport probably originated in Canada. It was popular in the 1930s, particularly in the United

States, but declined as a sport when skiing gained in popularity. It is a pastime much enjoyed by children.

Walking

Often called the 'heel and toe' sport, because the early method of judging the fairness of competitors laid emphasis on these as points of contact with the ground.

Walking is used as a test of fitness, and there have been some remarkable results in speed and endurance. Its popularity as a sport dates from the latter part of the 19th century – between 1850 and 1870 records were set up mainly as the result of a staked wager. Walking races first became a part of the Olympic games in 1908.

Water Polo

A game of 'football in the water' was proposed in 1870, but it was not until ten or so years later that the first organized game, similar to the modern one, was played.

Water polo is played by two teams of seven players each, in indoor and outdoor pools.

Interest in water polo both as a player and spectator sport increased with international competition, especially in Europe and Central and South America. It requires only limited space and inexpensive facilities and equipment.

Wrestling

One of the most primitive and universal of sports. A contest in which two people try to throw each other to the ground. Sculptures on Temple tombs in the Nile valley depict wrestling matches, showing nearly all the holds known today, proving that wrestling was a highly developed sport in at least 3000 BC.

The sport may have been introduced into Greece from Egypt or Asia, though Greek tradition ascribes its invention to the legendary hero, Theseus.

Wrestling was an important branch of athletics in ancient Greece. It was one of the events at the 18th Olympiad, about 704 BC. The most famous wrestler of ancient times was Milo of Croton (c. 520 BC), who scored 32 victories in the different national games, six of them at Olympia.

English literature is full of references to the sport – Henry VIII is known to have been a strong wrestler. It is now enjoyed as a spectator sport by millions through the medium of television.

There are various styles of wrestling, that prevailing in the north of England and the south of Scotland is known as the Cumberland style. Until recently there was a difference between the styles of Cornwall and Devon, the wrestlers of Devon having worn heavily soled shoes. The Lancashire style of wrestling, known as Catch-as-catch-can, is popular not only throughout Great Britain generally, but also in the United States, Canada, Australia, Switzerland and other countries. It is the legitimate descendant of the ancient Greek upright wrestling. The national style in Ireland is called Collar and elbow.

Continental wrestlers chiefly favour the Graeco-Roman style which is far more restricted and less free, the bouts consisting mainly of struggles on the ground.

13 MEDICINE

The Hippocratic Oath

Hippocrates, the 'father of medicine', was born on the island of Cos off the coast of Asia Minor in about 460 B C. Little is known of his life except that he taught and practised medicine in Cos and other parts of Greece and died at a great age.

Stethoscopes and thermometers were not then known, and Hippocrates used his own powers of observation and logical reasoning to diagnose disease. His abilities as a physician were venerated by medical men in the ages which followed. The oath of Hippocrates, an appeal for correct conduct, was perhaps the greatest legacy he left to the medical profession. It has been adopted by medical men as an ethical code or ideal – it is not a law. It is still used during the graduation ceremony at certain universities and schools of medicine. It runs as follows:

'I will look upon him who shall have taught me this Art even as one of my parents. I will share my substance with him, and I will supply his necessities, if he be in need. I will regard his offspring even as my own brethren, and I will teach them this Art, if they would learn it, without fee or covenant. I will impart this Art by precept, by lecture and by every mode of teaching, not only to my own sons but to the sons of him who has taught me, and to disciples bound by covenant and oath, according to the Law of Medicine.

'The regimen I adopt shall be for the benefit of my patients according to my ability and judgement, and not for their hurt or for any wrong. I will give no deadly drug to any, though it be asked of me, nor will I counsel

such, and especially I will not aid a woman to procure abortion. Whatsoever house I enter, there will I go for the benefit of the sick, refraining
from all wrong doing or corruption, and especially from any act of
seduction, of male or female, of bond or free. Whatsoever things I see
or hear concerning the life of men, in my attendance on the sick or even
apart therefrom, which ought not to be noised abroad, I will keep silence
thereon, counting such things to be as sacred secrets.'

Medical Note

> Normal Pulse Rate – 72 per minute
> Normal Breathing – 15–18 respirations per minute
> Normal Body Temperature – 98·4°F.

BRIEF NURSING GLOSSARY

Abrasion – superficial injury: scraping of the skin
Ampoule – small sealed glass phial containing a drug
Antibiotic – a substance, derived from fungi or moulds, used to treat infection
Antiseptic – a substance which inhibits the growth of bacteria
Bacteria – minute living creatures. Many are beneficial, but many cause disease
Calorie – amount of heat required to raise 1 kg of water through 1° C. Used as a unit to estimate the energy value of food
Chiropody – treatment of foot conditions
Deodorant – a substance which masks or destroys an unpleasant smell
Diagnosis – identification of the disease from which the patient is suffering
Dyspnoea – difficult breathing
Haemorrhage – loss of blood
Immunity – resistance to infection
Malaise – feeling of illness or discomfort
Narcotic – a drug which produces deep sleep
Occupational Therapy – occupations for treatment in either physical or mental illness
Paediatrics – branch of medicine dealing with children
Physiotherapy – treatment with physical measures, such as heat, light, massage and exercise
Radiograph – an X-ray picture
Sphygmomanometer – apparatus for measuring blood pressure
X-rays – short rays of the electromagnetic spectrum, used for diagnosis or treatment

Discoveries and Innovations in
Chemistry, Physics, Biology and Medicine

Invention/Discovery	Name	Nationality	Date
Adrenalin	Takamine	Japanese	1901
Antiseptic surgery	Lister	English	1867
Aspirin	Dreser	German	1889
Atomic Theory	Dalton	English	1803
Bleaching Powder	Tennant	English	1798
Chloroform	Guthrie, S.	American	1831
Cocaine	Niemann	German	1860
Cosmic Rays	Gockel	Swiss	1910
Cyanide	Caro, Frank	German	1905
Evolution (Natural Selection)	Darwin	English	1858
Human Heart Transplant	Barnard	S. African	1967
Insulin	Banting, Best, MacLeod	Canadian	1922
Neutron	Chadwick	English	1932
Oxygen	Priestley	English	1774
Penicillin	Fleming	Scottish	1929
Radioactivity	Becquerel	French	1896
Radium	Curie, Pierre	French	1896
Streptomycin	Waksman	American	1945
Sulphuric Acid	Phillips	English	1831
Uranium fission (atomic reactor)	Enrico Fermi, Leo Szilard	Italian, American	1942

Invention/Discovery	Name	Nationality	Date
Vitamin A	McCollum, Davis	American	1913
Vitamin B	McCollum	American	1916
Vitamin C	Holst, Froelich	Norwegian	1912
Vitamin D	McCollum	American	1922

Great Inventions and Scientific Discoveries

Invention/Discovery	Name	Date
Adding Machine	Blaise Pascal (France)	1642
Air Conditioning	Willis H. Carrier (USA)	1911
Balloon	Jacques and Joseph Montgolfier (France)	1783
Barometer	Evangelista Torricelli (Italy)	1643
Bicycle	Kirkpatrick Macmillan (Scotland)	1839
Bifocal lens	Benjamin Franklin (USA)	1780
Car (Internal combustion)	Jean Joseph Etienne Lenoir (France)	Patented 1860
Car (Petrol driven)	Karl-Friedrich Benz (Ger.)	Patented 1886
Cash Register	James Ritty (USA)	1879
Cathode Ray Tube	Karl Ferdinand Braun (Ger.)	1897 (first commercial use)
Cement	L. J. Vicat (France)	1824 (invented cement made from chalk and clay)
Clock (Earliest mechanical)	I'Hsing and Liang Ling-tsan (China)	Completed AD 725
Clock (Pendulum)	Christian Huygens (Holland)	1657
Dynamite	Alfred Nobel (Sweden)	Invented 1867
Dynamo	Antonio Picinotti (Italy)	1860
Electric lamp	Thomas Alva Edison (USA)	1879
Electronic Computer	J. G. Brainerd, J. P. Eckert, J. W. Manchly (USA)	1942
Gas Turbine Engine	John Barber (England)	1791

Invention/Discovery	Name	Date
Gear (Differential)	Onésiphore Pecquer (France)	Invented 1828
Gramophone (Phonograph)	Thomas Alva Edison (USA)	Patented 1878
Gyro compass	Elmer Sperry (USA)	1911
Hovercraft	Sir Christopher Cockerell (Britain)	Patented 1955
Incubator	Cornelius Drebbel (Holland)	1666 (Patented by John Champion of London 1770)
Jet engine	Sir Frank Whittle (England)	1929 (An engine similar to Whittle's was patented by a Frenchman, Guillaume in 1900. Earliest test-bed run, 1937)
Lifeboat	Henry Greathead (England)	Invented 1789 (Patent granted to Lukin, 1785)
Lightning conductor	Benjamin Franklin (USA)	Invented 1752
Long-playing Record	Dr Peter Goldmark (USA)	First introduced 1948
Magnetic Recording	Vlademar Poulsen (Denmark)	Patent filed 1898
Margarine	Hippolyte Mège-Mouries (France)	1863
Match (Safety)	J. E. Lundstrom (Sweden)	1855
Microphone	Alexander Graham Bell (USA)	1876
Microscope	Zacharias Janssen (Netherlands)	1590
Nylon	Dr Wallace H. Carothers (USA)	1937
Parking Meter	Carl C. Magee (USA)	Installed in Oklahoma, USA, 1935
Passenger lift	Elisha G. Otis (USA)	1852
Piano	Bartolommeo Cristofori (Italy)	Earliest in existence, 1720

Invention/Discovery	Name	Date
Radar	Robert Watson-Watt (Britain)	1935
Radio	Guglielmo Marconi (Italy/Ireland)	1896 (First patent for a system of communication by means of electro-magnetic waves)
Rayon	Sir Joseph Swan (Britain)	1883
Rubber (latex foam)	E. A. Murphy (Britain)	1928
Rubber (vulcanized)	Charles Goodyear (USA)	1841
Safety pin	William Hunt (USA)	1849
Safety razor	William Samuel Henson (England)	1847
Telegraph	William Coke, Charles Wheatstone (Britain)	1837
Telephone	{ J. Philip Reis (Germany)	1861
	Alexander Graham Bell (USA)	1876
Telescope (Refracting)	Johannes Lippershey (Netherlands)	1608
Terylene	J. R. Whinfield, J. T. Dickson (England)	1941
Thermometer	Galileo Galilei (Italy)	1593
Transistor	Shockley, Britain and Bardeen (USA)	1947
Typewriter	Austin Burt (USA)	Invented 1829 (First patented by Henry Mill, 1744)
Zip fastener	Whitcomb L. Judson (USA)	Patent issued 1891

THE EARLIEST CROSSWORD PUZZLE was invented by Liverpool-born Arthur Wynne, and published in the 'New York World' on December 21st, 1913.

THE LARGEST CROSSWORD PUZZLE – with over 3,000 clues down and over 3,000 clues across was compiled, in his spare time, by Robert M. Stilgenbauer. It took him 7½ years.

Chemical Elements

All known matter in the Solar System is made up of chemical elements. An element in chemistry is any substance that cannot be separated by chemical means into simpler substances. One hundred and four naturally occurring elements have been detected so far. They are listed in the following table.

Table of Chemical Elements

Element	Chemical Symbol	Atomic Number	Atomic Weight	Element	Chemical Symbol	Atomic Number	Atomic Weight
Actinium	Ac	89	227	Cadmium	Cd	48	112·4
Aluminium	Al	13	27	Caesium	Cs	55	132·9
Americium	Am	95	243	Calcium	Ca	20	40·1
Antimony	Sb	51	121·8	Californium	Cf	98	251
Argon	Ar	18	39·9	Carbon	C	6	12
Arsenic	As	33	74·9	Cerium	Ce	58	140·1
Astatine	At	85	210	Chlorine	Cl	17	35·5
Barium	Ba	56	137·3	Chromium	Cr	24	52
Berkelium	Bk	97	249	Cobalt	Co	27	58·9
Beryllium	Be	4	9	Copper	Cu	29	63·5
Bismuth	Bi	83	209	Curium	Cm	96	247
Boron	B	5	10·8	Dysprosium	Dy	66	162·5
Bromine	Br	35	79·9	Einsteinium	Es	99	254

Element	Chemical Symbol	Atomic Number	Atomic Weight	Element	Chemical Symbol	Atomic Number	Atomic Weight
Erbium	Er	68	167·3	Phosphorus	P	15	31
Europium	Eu	63	152	Platinum	Pt	78	195·1
Fermium	Fm	100	253	Plutonium	Pu	94	242
Fluorine	F	9	19	Polonium	Po	84	210
Francium	Fr	87	223	Potassium	K	19	39·1
Gadolinium	Gd	64	157·3	Praseodymium	Pr	59	140·9
Gallium	Ga	31	69·7	Promethium	Pm	61	147
Germanium	Ge	32	72·6	Protactinium	Pa	91	231
Gold	Au	79	197	Radium	Ra	88	226
Hafnium	Hf	72	178·5	Radon	Rn	86	222
Helium	He	2	4	Rhenium	Re	75	186·2
Holmium	Ho	67	164·9	Rhodium	Rh	45	102·9
Hydrogen	H	1	1	Rubidium	Rb	37	85·5
Indium	In	49	114·8	Ruthenium	Ru	44	101·1
Iodine	I	53	126·9	Samarium	Sm	62	150·4
Iridium	Ir	77	192·2	Scandium	Sc	21	45
Iron	Fe	26	55·8	Selenium	Se	34	79
Krypton	Kr	36	83·8	Silicon	Si	14	28·1
Kurchatovium	Ku	104	260	Silver	Ag	47	107·9
Lanthanum	La	57	138·9	Sodium	Na	11	23
Lawrencium	Lw	103	257	Strontium	Sr	38	87·6
Lead	Pb	82	207·2	Sulphur	S	16	32·1
Lithium	Li	3	6·9	Tantalum	Ta	73	180·9
Lutetium	Lu	71	175	Technetium	Tc	43	99
Magnesium	Mg	12	24·3	Tellurium	Te	52	127·6
Manganese	Mn	25	54·9	Terbium	Tb	65	158·9
Mendelevium	Md	101	256	Thallium	Tl	81	204·4
Mercury	Hg	80	200·6	Thorium	Th	90	232
Molybdenum	Mo	42	95·9	Thulium	Tm	69	168·9
Neodymium	Nd	60	144·2	Tin	Sn	50	118·7
Neon	Ne	10	20·2	Titanium	Ti	22	47·9
Neptunium	Np	93	237	Tungsten	W	74	183·9
Nickel	Ni	28	58·7	Uranium	U	92	238
Niobium	Nb	41	92·9	Vanadium	V	23	50·9
Nitrogen	N	7	14	Xenon	Xe	54	131·3
Nobelium	No	102	254	Ytterbium	Yb	70	173
Osmium	Os	76	190·2	Yttrium	Y	39	88·9
Oxygen	O	8	16	Zinc	Zn	30	65·4
Palladium	Pd	46	106·4	Zirconium	Zr	40	91·2

Relative Densities of Common Substances

Gases (*at Normal Temperature & Pressure*)

Air	0·00129
Argon	0·00178
Carbon dioxide	0·00198
Helium	0·000179
Hydrogen	0·00009
Methane	0·000717
Oxygen	0·00143

Liquids (*at 15°C*)

Acetone	0·79
Alcohol	0·79
Ether	0·74
Glycerine	1·26
Oil (lubricating)	0·9–0·92
Turpentine	0·87
Blood	1·04–1·067
(Water at 4°C)	1·00

Metals

Steel	7·6–7·8
Brass	8·4–8·7
Aluminium	2·70
Copper	8·89
Lead	11·34
Titanium	4·5
Mercury	13·6

Miscellaneous Solids

Celluloid	1·4
Glass	2·4–2·8
Ice	0·92
Brick	2·1
Diamond	3·5
Rubber	0·97–0·99
Oak	0·74
Cork	0·24

Specific Heats of Common Substances

Aluminium	0·202
Brass	0·092
Copper	0·093
Iron	0·113
Rubber	0·400
Wood	0·400

Alcohol	0·580
Chloroform	0·234
Air	0·241*
Carbon dioxide	0·202*
Oxygen	0·218*
Water	1·000
(*at constant pressure)	

Air

Normal dry air has the following composition by volume:

	%		%
Nitrogen	78·08	Helium	0·0005
Oxygen	20·94	Krypton	0·0001
Argon	0·9325	Xenon	0·000009
Carbon dioxide	0·03	Radon	6×10^{-18}
Neon	0·0018		

Chemical and Common Names of Some Familiar Substances

Alum	Potassium aluminium sulphate (K_2SO_4, $Al_2(SO_4)_3$, $24H_2O$).
Aqua fortis	Concentrated nitric acid (HNO_3).
Aqua regia	Concentrated nitric and hydrochloric acids in ratio of one part HNO_3 to four parts HCl.
Boracic acid	Boric acid (H_3BO_3).
Borax	Sodium pyroborate ($Na_2B_4O_7$).
Bromide	Potassium bromide (KBr).
Carbolic acid	Phenol (C_6H_5OH).
Carbonic acid gas	Carbon dioxide (CO_2).
Caustic soda	Sodium hydroxide (NaOH).
Chalk	Calcium carbonate ($CaCO_3$).
Common salt	Sodium chloride (NaCl).
Epsom salt	Crystalline magnesium sulphate ($MgSO_4$, $7H_2O$).
Hypo	Sodium thiosulphate ($Na_2S_2O_3$).
Lime	Calcium oxide (CaO).
Magnesia	Magnesium oxide (MgO).
Muriate of potash	Potassium chloride (KCl).
Nitre	Potassium nitrate (KNO_3).
Oil of vitriol	Concentrated sulphuric acid (H_2SO_4).
Plaster of Paris	Form of calcium sulphate having the formula $CaSO_4, \frac{1}{2}H_2O$.

Potash	Potassium carbonate (K_2CO_3).
Quicklime	Calcium oxide (CaO).
Red lead	Red lead oxide (Pb_3O_4).
Saltpetre	Potassium nitrate (KNO_3).
Salts of lemon	Potassium hydrogen oxalate ($KH_3(OOC)_4$, $2H_2O$).
Sal volatile	Ammonium carbonate ($(NH_4)_2CO_3$).
Slaked lime	Calcium hydroxide ($Ca(OH)_2$).
Spirits of salt	Solution of hydrochloric acid (HCl).
Vinegar	Solution of acetic acid (CH_3COOH).
Vitriol (Blue)	Crystalline copper sulphate ($CuSO_4$, $5H_2O$).
(Green)	Crystalline ferrous sulphate ($FeSO_4$, $7H_2O$).
Washing soda	Crystalline sodium carbonate ($Na_2CO_31OH_2O$).

Some Abbreviations in Common Use in Chemistry and Physics

a	Acid	eth.	Ether
a.c.	Alternating current	exp.	Explodes
al.	Alcohol	fl.	Fluid
aq.	Aqua; water	glyc.	Glycerine
atm. *or*	Atmosphere	hor.	Horizontal
atmos.	(Atmospheric)	i.	Insoluble
av. *or* avoir.	Avoirdupois	km.	Kilometre
bar.	Barometer	kw.	Kilowatt
b.p.	Boiling point	lat.	Latitude
cc *or* c.c.	Cubic centimetre	mg.	Milligram
chl.	Chloroform	mic.	Microscopic
cm.	Centimetre	mm.	Millimetre
cu. ft.	Cubic foot	m.p.	Melting point
cwt.	Hundredweight	oz.	Ounce
d.c.	Direct current	pr.	Prisms
diam.	Diameter	Q.	Quantity
dil.	Dilute	r.p.m.	Revolutions per
dissd.	Dissolved		minute
dr.	Dram	sc.	Scales
dwt.	Pennyweight	sol.	Solution; Soluble

sp. gr.	Specific gravity	**w.**	Water
sq.	Square	**wt.**	Weight
t.	Troy	**yr.**	Year
temp.	Temperature		
turp.	Turpentine		

Mathematical Formulae

To find the area of a:

CIRCLE – Multiply the square of the diameter by ·7854
RECTANGLE – Multiply the length of the base by the height
SQUARE – Square the length of one side
TRIANGLE – Multiply the base by the height and divide by 2.

Mathematical Signs

$=$	Is equal to	$\not>$	Not greater than
$\neq$	Is not equal to	$<$	Less than
$\risingdotseq$	Is approx. equal to	$\not<$	Not less than
$\equiv$	Is identical to	Σ	The sum of
$\sim$	The difference between	δ	A small difference
$\propto$	Varies as	$\angle$	Angle
$>$	Greater than	∞	Infinity

60 seconds ($''$) = 1 minute ($'$)   90 degrees = 1 right angle
60 minutes = 1 degree ($°$)   4 right angles = 1 circle (360°)

British Measures and Equivalents

Length

1 inch	2·54 cm.
1 foot = 12 inches	0·3048 m.
1 yard = 3 feet	0·9144 m.
1 chain = 4 rods = 22 yards	20·1168 m.
1 mile = 8 furlongs = 80 chains	1·6093 km.
1 nautical mile = 6,080 feet	1·852 km.

Surface or Area

1 sq. inch	6·4516 sq. cm.
1 sq. foot = 144 sq. inch	9·2903 sq. dm.
1 sq. yard = 9 sq. feet	0·836 sq. m.
1 acre = 4 roods = 4,840 sq. yards	4,046·556 sq. m.
1 sq. mile = 640 acres	258·99 hectares

Capacity

1 cu. inch	16·387 cu. cm.
1 cu. foot = 1,728 cu. inch	28·317 cu. dm.
1 cu. yard = 27 cu. feet	0·7646 cu. m.
1 pint = 4 gills	0·568 litres
1 gallon = 4 quarts = 8 pints	4·546 litres
1 bushel = 4 pecks = 8 gallons	36·368 litres

Weight

1 ounce = 16 drams = 437·5 grains	28·35 gm.
1 pound = 16 ounces	0·4536 kg.
1 stone = 14 pounds	6·35 kg.
1 hundredweight = 4 quarters = 8 stones	0·5080 quintal
1 ton = 20 hundredweight	1·016 tonnes

Metric Measures and Equivalents

Length

1 centimetre (cm.) = 10 millimetres (mm.)	0·3937 in.
1 metre (m.) = 100 centimetres	1·094 yd.
1 kilometre (km.) = 1,000 metres	0·62137 mile

(A kilometre is approximately *five-eighths* of a mile, so that 8 kilometres may be regarded as 5 miles.)

Surface or Area

1 sq. centimetre = 100 sq. mm.	0·155 sq. in.
1 sq. metre = 10,000 sq. cm.	1,196 sq. yd.
1 are = 100 sq. m.	119·6 sq. yd.
1 hectare = 100 ares	2·4711 acres
1 sq. kilometre = 100 hectares	0·386103 sq. mile

Capacity
1 cu. centimetre | 0·061 cu. in.
1 cu. metre = 999·972 litres | 1·30795 cu. yd.
1 litre = 1·000028 cu. dm. | 1·7598 pint

Weight
1 milligram (mg.) | 0·015 grain
1 gramme (g.) = 1,000 milligrams | 15·432 grains
1 kilogram (kg.) = 1,000 grammes | 2·2046 lb.
1 quintal = 100 kilograms | 1·968 cwt.
1 tonne = 10 quintals | 0·9842 ton

World Currencies

Country	Monetary Unit	Denominations in Circulation	
		(Notes)	(Coins)
Albania	Lek of 100 Qindarka	Leks 100, 50, 25, 10, 5, 3, 1	Lek 1; Qintars 50, 20, 10, 5
Algeria	Dinar of 100 Centimes	Dinars 500, 100, 50, 10, 5	Dinars 5, 1; Centimes 50, 20, 10, 5, 2, 1
Argentina	Peso of 100 Centavos or 100 Old Pesos	Pesos 1,000, 500, 100, 50, 10, 5, 1. Old Pesos 10,000, 5,000, 1,000, 500, 100, 50	Old Pesos 25, 10, 5, 1; Centavos 50, 20, 10, 5, 1
Australia	Dollar of 100 Cents	$A 50, 20, 10, 5, 2, 1	Cents 50, 20, 10, 5, 2, 1
Austria	Schilling of 100 Groschen	Schillings 1,000, 500, 100, 50, 20	Schillings 50, 25, 10, 5, 1; Groschen 50, 10, 5, 2, 1
Belgium	Belgian Franc of 100 Centimes	Frs. 5,000, 1,000, 500, 100, 50, 20	Frs. 100, 50, 10, 5, 1; Centimes 50, 25
Brazil	Cruzeiro of 100 Centavos	Cruzeiros 500, 100, 50, 10, 5, 1	Cruzeiros 300, 20, 1; Centavos 50, 20, 10, 5, 2, 1

Country	Monetary Unit	Denominations in Circulation	
		(Notes)	(Coins)
Bulgaria	Lev of 100 Stotinki	Léva 20, 10, 5, 2, 1	Léva 2, 1; Stotinki 50, 20, 10, 5, 2, 1
Burma	Kyat of 100 Pyas	Kyats 20, 10, 5, 1	Kyat 1; Pyas 50, 25, 10, 5, 1
Canada	Dollar of 100 Cents	Dollars 1,000, 100, 50, 20, 10, 5, 2, 1	Dollars 1; Cents 50, 25, 10, 5, 1
Chile	Escudo of 100 Centésimos (=1,000 Pesos)	Escudos 5,000, 1,000, 500, 100, 50, 10, 5, 1, 0·50	Centésimos 10, 5, 1, ½
China	Renminbi or Yuan of 10 Jiao or 100 Fen	Yuan 10, 5, 2, 1; Jiao 5, 2, 1	Fen 5, 2, 1
Cuba	Peso of 100 Centavos	Pesos 100, 50, 20, 10, 5, 1	Centavos 40, 20, 5, 2, 1
Cyprus	Cyprus Pound of 1,000 Mils	£5, £1; Mils 500, 250	Mils 500, 100, 50, 25, 5, 3, 1
Czechoslo-vakia	Koruna (Crown) of 100 Haléřů (Heller)	Korunas 500, 100, 50, 20, 10	Korunas 5, 2, 1; Heller 50, 20, 10, 5, 3, 1
Denmark	Krone of 100 Ore	Kroner 500, 100, 50, 10	Kroner 5, 1; Ore 25, 10, 5
Ethiopia	Ethiopian Dollar of 100 Cents	Dollars 500, 100, 50, 20, 10, 5, 1	Cents 50, 25, 10, 5, 1
Finland	Markka of 100 Penniä	Markkas 100, 50, 10, 5, 1	Markkas 1; Penniä 50, 20, 10, 5, 1
Formosa	New Taiwan Dollar of 100 Cents	NT$ 100, 50, 10, 5	$5, $1; Cents 50, 20, 10
France	Franc of 100 Centimes (1 Franc = 100 old Francs)	Francs 500, 100, 50, 10	Francs 10, 5, 1, ½; Centimes 20, 10, 5, 1
Gambia	Dalasi of 100 Bututs	Dalasis 25, 10, 5, 1	Dalasi 1; Bututs 50, 25, 10, 5, 1

Country	Monetary Unit	Denominations in Circulation (Notes)	(Coins)
Germany (East)	Mark der Deutschen Demokratischen Republik (M.) of 100 Pfennig	M. 100, 50, 20, 10, 5	M. 20, 10, 5, 2, 1; Pfennig 50, 20, 10, 5, 1
Germany (Federal Republic of)	Deutsche Mark of 100 Pfennig	D.M. 1,000, 500, 100, 50, 20, 10, 5	D.M. 10, 5, 2, 1; Pfennig 50, 10, 5, 2, 1
Greece	Drachma of 100 Lepta	Drachmae 1,000, 500, 100, 50	Drachmae 20, 10, 5, 2, 1; Lepta 50, 20, 10, 5
Guyana	Guyana Dollar of 100 Cents	Dollars 20, 10, 5, 1	Cents 100, 50, 25, 10, 5, 1
Hungary	Forint of 100 Fillér	Forints 500, 100, 50, 20, 10	Forints 10, 5, 2, 1; Fillér 50, 20, 10, 5, 2
Iceland	Króna of 100 Aurar	Króna 5,000, 1,000, 500, 100	Króna 50, 10, 5, 1; Aurar 50, 10
India	Rupee of 100 Paise	Rupiahs 10,000, 5,000, 1,000, 500, 100, 50, 25, 10, 5, 2½, 1; Sen 50, 25, 10, 5, 1	Rupiahs 100, 50, 25, 10, 5, 2, 1
Indonesia	Rupiah of 100 Sen	Rupiahs 10,000, 5,000, 1,000, 500, 100, 50, 25, 10, 5, 2½, 1; Sen 50, 25, 10, 5, 1	Rupiahs 10, 5, 2, 1
Iran	Rial of 100 Dinars	Rials 10,000, 5,000, 1,000, 500, 200, 100, 50, 20, 10	Rials 20, 10, 5, 2, 1
Iraq	Iraqi Dinar of 1,000 Fils	Dinars 10, 5, 1, ½, ¼	Dinars 5, 1; Fils 500, 250, 100, 50, 25, 10, 5, 1

Country	Monetary Unit	Denominations in Circulation (Notes)	(Coins)
Israel	Israel Pound of 100 Agorot (formerly 1,000 Prutot)	Pounds 100, 50, 10, 5, 1, $\frac{1}{2}$; Prutot 500, 250, 100, 50	Pounds 1, $\frac{1}{2}$; Agorot 25, 10, 5, 1; Prutot 250, 100, 50, 25, 10, 5, 1
Italy	Lira	Lire 100,000, 50,000, 10,000, 5,000, 1,000, 500	Lire 1,000, 500, 100, 50, 20, 10, 5, 2, 1
Jamaica	Jamaican Dollar of 100 Cents	$10, 5, 2, 1; Cents 50	$1; Cents 50, 25, 20, 10, 5, 1
Japan	Yen	Yen 10,000, 5,000, 1,000, 500, 100	Yen 1,000, 100, 50, 10, 5, 1
Kenya	Kenya Shilling of 100 Cents	Shillings 100, 50, 20, 10, 5	Shillings 2, 1; Cents 50, 25, 10, 5
Kuwait	Kuwaiti Dinar of 1,000 Fils	Dinars 10, 5, 1, $\frac{1}{2}$, $\frac{1}{4}$	Fils 100, 50, 20, 10, 5, 1
Laos	Kip of 100 Ats	Kips 1,000, 500, 200, 50, 20, 10, 5, 1	—
Lebanon	Lebanese Pound of 100 Piastres	Pounds 100, 50, 25, 10, 5, 1	Piastres 50, 25, 10, 5, 2$\frac{1}{2}$, 1
Luxembourg	Franc of 100 Centimes	Francs 100, 50, 20, 10	Francs 250, 100, 10, 5, 1; Centimes 25
Malagasy Republic	Franc Malgache (F.M.G.)	Frs. 5,000, 1,000, 500	Frs. 20, 10, 5, 2, 1
Malaysia	Malaysian Dollar (Ringit) of 100 cents	Dollars 1,000, 100, 50, 10, 5, 1	Dollar 1; Cents 50, 20, 10, 5, 1
Mexico	Peso of 100 Centavos	Pesos 10,000, 1,000, 500, 100, 50, 20, 10, 5, 1	Pesos 25, 10, 5, 1; Centavos 50, 20, 10, 5, 1
Mongolian People's Republic	Tugrik of 100 Mongo	Tugriks 100, 50, 25, 10, 3, 1	Tugrik 1; Mongo 50, 20, 15, 10, 2, 1

Country	Monetary Unit	Denominations in Circulation (Notes)	(Coins)
Morocco	Dirham of 100 Centimes	Dirham 100, 50, 10, 5	Dirham 5; Centimes 50, 20, 10, 5, 2, 1
Mozambique	Escudo of 100 Centavos	Escudos 1,000, 500, 100, 50	Escudos 20, 10, 5, 2½, 1; Centavos 50, 20, 10
Nepal	Rupee of 100 Paisa	Rupees 1,000, 500, 100, 10, 5, 1	Rupee 1; Paisa 50, 25, 10, 5, 2, 1
Netherlands (The)	Florin (Guilder) of 100 Cents	Florins 1,000, 100, 25, 10, 5, 2½, 1	Florins 10, 2½, 1; Cents 25, 10, 5, 1
Netherlands Antilles (The)	N.A. Guilder of 100 Cents	Guilders 500, 250, 100, 50, 25, 10, 5, 2½, 1	Guilders 2½, 1, ¼, 1/10; Cents 5, 2½, 1
New Zealand	New Zealand Dollar of 100 Cents	N.Z. $ 100, 20, 10, 5, 2, 1	Cents 50, 20, 10, 5, 2, 1
Norway	Krone of 100 Ore	Kroner 1,000, 500, 100, 50, 10, 5	Kroner 5, 1; Ore 50, 25, 10, 5, 2, 1
Paraguay	Guarani of 100 Centimes	Guaranies 10,000, 5,000, 1,000, 500, 100, 50, 10, 5, 1	—
Peru	Gold Sol of 100 Centavos	Soles 1,000, 500, 200, 100, 50, 10, 5	Soles 10, 5, 1; Centavos 50, 25, 10, 5,
Philippines	Philippine Peso of 100 Centavos	Pesos 100, 50, 20, 10, 5	Peso 1; Centavos 50, 25, 10, 5, 1
Poland	Zloty of 100 Groszy	Zlotys 1,000, 500, 100, 50, 20	Zlotys 100, 50, 10, 5, 2, 1; Groszy 50, 20, 10, 5, 2, 1
Portugal	Escudo of 100 Centavos	Escudos 1,000, 500, 100, 50, 20	Escudos 50, 20, 10, 5, 2½, 1; Centavos 50, 20, 10

Country	Monetary Unit	Denominations in Circulation (Notes)	(Coins)
Rumania	Leu of 100 Bani	Lei 100, 50, 25, 10, 5, 3, 1	Lei 3, 1; Bani 25, 15, 10, 5, 3, 1
Saudi Arabia	Riyal of 20 Qursh or 100 Halalas	Riyals 100, 50, 10, 5, 1	Qursh 4, 2, 1; Halala 50, 25, 10, 5, 1
Seychelles	Rupee of 100 Cents	Rs. 100, 50, 20, 10, 5	Rupee 5, 1; Cents 50, 25, 5, 1
Sierra Leone	Leone of 100 Cents	Leone 5, 2, 1 Cents 50	Cents 50, 20, 10, 5, 1, $\frac{1}{2}$
Singapore	S. Dollar of 100 Cents	$1,000, 500, 100, 50, 25, 10 ,5, 1	$1; Cents 50, 20, 10, 5, 1
South Africa (Republic of)	Rand of 100 Cents	Rands 20, 10, 5, 2, 1; £SA 100, 20, 10, 5, 1; 10s.	Rand 1; Cents 50, 20, 10, 5, 2, 1, $\frac{1}{2}$
Spain	Peseta of 100 Céntimos	Pesetas 1,000, 500, 100,	Pesetas 100, 50, 25, 5, 2$\frac{1}{2}$, 1; Céntimos 50, 10
Sudan	Sudanese Pound of 100 Piastres or 1,000 Milliemes	£S 10, 5, 1; Piastres 50, 25	Piastres 10, 5, 2; Milliemes 10, 5, 2, 1
Sweden	Krona of 100 Ore	Kronor 10,000, 1,000, 100, 50, 10, 5	Kronor 10, 5, 2, 1; Ore 50, 25, 10, 5, 2, 1
Switzerland	Franc of 100 Centimes	Francs 1,000, 500, 100, 50, 20, 10, 5	Francs 5, 2, 1; Centimes 50, 20, 10, 5, 2, 1
Thailand	Baht of 100 Stangs	Bahts 100, 20, 10, 5, 1; Stangs 50	Baht 1; Stangs 50, 25, 20, 10, 5, 1, $\frac{1}{2}$
Tonga	Pa'anga (T$) of 100 Seniti	Pa'anga 10, 5, 2, 1, $\frac{1}{2}$	Pa'anga 2, 1; Seniti 50, 20, 10, 5, 2, 1
Trinidad & Tobago	Trinidad & Tobago Dollar of 100 Cents	Dollars 20, 10, 5, 1	Dollar 1; Cents 50, 25, 10, 5, 1
Tunisia	Tunisian Dinar of 1,000 Millimes	Dinars 10, 5, 1, $\frac{1}{2}$	Dinar $\frac{1}{2}$; Millimes 100, 50, 20, 10, 5, 2, 1

Country	Monetary Unit	Denominations in Circulation (Notes)	(Coins)
Turkey	Turkish Lira of 100 Kurus	TL 1,000, 500, 100, 50, 20, 10, 5	TL 10, 5, 2, 1; Kurus 50, 25, 10, 5, 1
Uganda	U. Shilling of 100 Cents	Shillings 100, 50, 20, 10	Shillings 5, 2, 1; Cents 50, 20, 10, 5
United Arab Emirates	Dirham of 100 Fils	Dirhams 100, 50, 10, 5, 1	Dirham 1; Fils 50, 25, 10, 5, 1
United Kingdom	Pound of 100 new pence	£20, £10, £5, £1	Pence 50, 10, 5, 2, 1, $\frac{1}{2}$; 5s (25p); 6d ($2\frac{1}{2}$p)
United States of America	Dollar of 100 Cents	$100, 50, 20, 10, 5, 1	$1; Cents 50, 25, 10, 5, 1
Uruguay	Peso of 100 Centésimos	Pesos 10,000, 5,000, 1,000, 500, 100, 50	Pesos 1,000, 50, 20, 10, 5, 1
USSR	Rouble of 100 Copecks	Roubles 100, 50, 25, 10, 5, 3, 1	Rouble 1; Copecks 50, 20, 15, 10, 5, 3, 2, 1
Venezuela	Bolivar	Bolivares 500, 100, 50, 20, 10, 5	Bolivares 100, 20, 10, 5, 2, 1, $\frac{1}{2}$, $\frac{1}{4}$, $\frac{1}{8}$, $\frac{1}{20}$
Vietnam (North)	Dong of 10 Hào or 100 Xu	Dong 10, 5, 2, 1; Hào 5, 2, 1; Xu 2	Xu 5, 2, 1
Vietnam (South)	Dong of 100 Cents	Dong 1,000, 500, 200, 100, 50, 20, 10, 5, 1	Dong 20, 10, 5, 1
Yemen (Arab Republic)	Riyal of 40 Bugshas	Riyals 50, 20, 10, 5, 1; Bugshas 20, 10	Bugshas 2, 1, $\frac{1}{2}$
Yemen (People's Democratic Republic)	Southern Yemen Dinar (YD) of 1,000 fils	YD 10, 5, 1; Fils 500, 250	Fils 50, 25, 5, 1

Country	Monetary Unit	Denominations in Circulation (Notes)	(Coins)
Yugoslavia	Dinar of 100 Paras	Dinars 500, 100, 50, 10, 5	Dinar 5, 2, 1; Paras 50, 20, 10, 5
Zambia	Kwacha of 100 Ngwee	Kwacha 20, 10, 5, 2, 1; Ngwee 50	Ngwee 50, 20, 10, 5, 2, 1

British Monetary Units in 1922

The authorized coinage of the United Kingdom in 1922 consisted of the following pieces:

Denomination	Standard Weight	Remedy of Weight**
Gold		
*Five Pound £5	616·37239	1·00
*Two Pound £2	246·54895	0·40
Sovereign £1	123·27447	0·20
Half-Sovereign 10s	61·63723	0·15
Silver		
Crown 5s	436·36363	2·000
Double Florin 4s	349·09090	1·678
Half-Crown 2s 6d	218·18181	1·264
Florin 2s	174·54545	0·997
Shilling 1s	87·27272	0·578
Sixpence 6d	43·63636	0·346
*Groat or 4d	29·09090	0·262
Threepence 3d	21·81818	0·212
*Twopence 2d	14·54545	0·144
*Penny 1d	7·27272	0·087

Denomination	Standard Weight	Remedy of Weight**
Bronze		
Penny 1*d*	145·83333	2·916
Halfpenny ½*d*	87·50000	1·750
Farthing ¼*d*	43·75000	0·875

*Issued on special occasions only.

**The 'Remedy' is the amount of variation from standard permitted in fineness and in weight of coins when first issued from the Mint.

British Monetary Units in 1977

COIN

Bronze Coins
½ New Penny
1 New Penny
2 New Pence

Cupro-Nickel (Silver)

Sixpence 6*d*	2½p
Shilling 1*s*	} 5p
5 New Pence	
Florin 2*s*	} 10p
10 New Pence	
Crown* 5*s*	25p
50 New Pence	50p

Silver Coins
The Maundy Money: gifts of special money distributed by the Sovereign annually to the number of aged poor people corresponding to the Sovereign's age.

Fourpence	4p
Threepence	3p
Twopence	2p
Penny	1p

*Gold Coins***

Five Pound	£5
Two Pound	£2
Sovereign	£1
Half-Sovereign	10*s*

*Legal tender but not in general circulation as collector's value greater than face value. Issued on special occasions mainly connected with the Royal Family.

**Discontinued.

BANK NOTES

Bank of England notes are issued in denominations of £1, £5, £10 and £20.

SIZES AND WEIGHTS OF DECIMAL COINS

Denomination	Metal	Standard Weight (Grams)	Standard Diameter (Centimetres)
New Halfpenny	Bronze	1·78200	1·7145
New Penny	Bronze	3·56400	2·0320
2 New Pence	Bronze	7·12800	2·5910
5 New Pence	Cupro-nickel	5·65518	2·3595
10 New Pence	Cupro-nickel	11·31036	2·8500
50 New Pence	Cupro-nickel	13·5	3

Premium Savings Bonds

Premium Savings Bonds were proposed by the then Chancellor of the Exchequer, Mr Harold Macmillan, in his budget of April 1956. They are a Government security and were put on sale on November 1st, 1956.

Premium Savings Bonds do not bear interest for individual holders. Instead, a sum equivalent to interest is pooled to form a fund, and distributed by weekly and monthly prize draws. A bond becomes eligible for a draw after it has been held for three complete calendar months; it remains eligible until the end of the month in which it is repaid or until the end of the twelfth month following the month in which the holder dies (bonds may be encashed at any time by the deceased's next-of-kin or legal representative).

Bonds are issued in 14 different values ranging from £5 to £500. Each £1 invested buys one bond unit and gives one chance in each of the prize draws for which the unit is eligible. The maximum permitted holding is 2,000 £1 units.

Winning numbers are selected by Electronic Random Number Indicator Equipment, popularly known as ERNIE. A new Ernie, introduced early in 1973, has the capability of generating the latest ten-character numbers and carries out the operation in a fraction of the time taken by the original equipment.

Ernie is electronic, but it may be helpful to think of a box containing ten wheels spinning erratically behind small windows. If the wheels are stopped simultaneously the numbers or letters around the rims can be read as a complete bond number.

The numbers generated by Ernie actually depend on the chance movement of electrons, caused by passing an electric current through a 'zener diode'. This produces, at irregular intervals, pulses of electrical energy which are counted electronically during a brief but constant period of time – actually 15 milliseconds. To make the randomness doubly sure the 'counts' from two diodes are combined to give each digit of the complete number.

Ten different pairings of diodes and counters operate simultaneously to make a complete number; letters are generated in the same way as the figures, the counters counting ABC . . . instead of 123. Earlier nine- or eight-character numbers are produced when the first, or first two, digits are generated by Ernie as 'O'.

The monthly prize fund is allocated in prizes as follows:

1. An amount is set aside to allow for a single £50,000 prize and 25 £1,000 prizes in each weekly draw, the number of such draws being equal to the number of Saturdays in the month;

2. The balance is allocated to the monthly draw as follows:

    i. A single prize of £100,000 and one of £25,000.

    ii. Of the remainder, each complete £100,000 is divided into:

1 prize of £5,000	25 prizes of £100
10 prizes of £1,000	1,000 prizes of £50
10 prizes of £500	1,100 prizes of £25

    iii. Each remaining £10,000 is divided into:

1 prize of £1,000	100 prizes of £50
1 prize of £500	100 prizes of £25
10 prizes of £100	

    iv. Any residue less than £10,000 is divided into £25 prizes.

By November 1976, the number of bondholders was estimated to be over 21 million and the net amount standing to their credit was almost £1,165 million. Since the inception of the scheme over 13 million prizes, valued at more than £550 million, has been paid out.

17 PRIME MINISTERS AND PRESIDENTS

British Prime Ministers

Name	Party	Date
Sir Robert Walpole	Whig	April 3rd, 1721
Earl of Wilmington	Whig	February 16th, 1742
Henry Pelham	Whig	August 25th, 1743
Duke of Newcastle	Whig	May 18th, 1754
Duke of Devonshire	Whig	November 16th, 1756
Duke of Newcastle	Whig	July 2nd, 1757
Earl of Bute	Tory	May 28th, 1762
George Grenville	Whig	April 15th, 1763
Marquess of Rockingham	Whig	July 10th, 1765
Earl of Chatham	Whig	August 2nd, 1766
Duke of Grafton	Whig	December 1767
Lord North	Tory	February 6th, 1770
Marquess of Rockingham	Whig	March 27th, 1782
Earl of Shelburne	Whig	July 13th, 1782
Duke of Portland	Coalition	April 4th, 1783
William Pitt	Tory	December 7th, 1783
Henry Addington	Tory	March 21st, 1801
William Pitt	Tory	May 16th, 1804
Lord Grenville	Whig	February 10th, 1806
Duke of Portland	Tory	March 31st, 1807
Spencer Perceval	Tory	December 6th, 1809
Earl of Liverpool	Tory	June 16th, 1812

Name	Party	Date
George Canning	Tory	April 30th, 1827
Viscount Goderich	Tory	September 8th, 1827
Duke of Wellington	Tory	January 26th, 1828
Earl Grey	Whig	November 24th, 1830
Viscount Melbourne	Whig	July 13th, 1834
Sir Robert Peel	Tory	December 26th, 1834
Viscount Melbourne	Whig	March 18th, 1835
Sir Robert Peel	Tory	September 6th, 1841
Lord John Russell	Whig	July 6th, 1846
Earl of Derby	Tory	February 28th, 1852
Earl of Aberdeen	Peelite	December 28th, 1852
Viscount Palmerston	Liberal	February 10th, 1855
Earl of Derby	Conservative	February 25th, 1858
Viscount Palmerston	Liberal	June 18th, 1859
Earl Russell	Liberal	November 6th, 1865
Earl of Derby	Conservative	July 6th, 1866
Benjamin Disraeli	Conservative	February 27th, 1868
W. E. Gladstone	Liberal	December 9th, 1868
Benjamin Disraeli	Conservative	February 21st, 1874
W. E. Gladstone	Liberal	April 28th, 1880
Marquess of Salisbury	Conservative	June 24th, 1885
W. E. Gladstone	Liberal	February 6th, 1886
Marquess of Salisbury	Conservative	August 3rd, 1886
W. E. Gladstone	Liberal	August 18th, 1892
Earl of Rosebery	Liberal	March 3rd, 1894
Marquess of Salisbury	Conservative	July 2nd, 1895
A. J. Balfour	Conservative	July 12th, 1902
Sir H. Campbell-Bannerman	Liberal	December 5th, 1905
H. H. Asquith	Liberal	April 8th, 1908
H. H. Asquith	Coalition	May 26th, 1915
D. Lloyd-George	Coalition	December 7th, 1916
A. Bonar Law	Conservative	October 23rd, 1922
Stanley Baldwin	Conservative	May 22nd, 1923
J. Ramsay MacDonald	Labour	January 22nd, 1924
Stanley Baldwin	Conservative	November 4th, 1924
J. Ramsay MacDonald	Labour	June 8th, 1929
J. Ramsay MacDonald	Coalition	August 25th, 1931
Stanley Baldwin	Coalition	June 7th, 1935
Neville Chamberlain	Coalition	May 28th, 1937
Winston S. Churchill	Coalition	May 11th, 1940

Name	Party	Date
Winston S. Churchill	Conservative	May 23rd, 1945
Clement R. Attlee	Labour	July 26th, 1945
Sir Winston S. Churchill	Conservative	October 26th, 1951
Sir Anthony Eden	Conservative	April 6th, 1955
Harold Macmillan	Conservative	January 13th, 1957
Sir Alec Douglas-Home	Conservative	October 19th, 1963
J. H. Wilson	Labour	October 16th, 1964
E. R. G. Heath	Conservative	June 19th, 1970
J. H. Wilson	Labour	February 28th, 1974
James Callaghan	Labour	April 5th, 1976

Presidents of the United States of America

Name	Party	Date
1. George Washington	Federalist	1789–97
2. John Adams	Federalist	1797–1801
3. Thomas Jefferson	Republican	1801–9
4. James Madison	Republican	1809–17
5. James Monroe	Republican	1817–25
6. John Quincy Adams	Republican	1825–29
7. Andrew Jackson	Democrat	1829–37
8. Martin Van Buren	Democrat	1837–41
9. William H. Harrison	Whig	1841
10. John Tyler	Whig	1841–45
11. James Knox Polk	Democrat	1845–49
12. Zachary Taylor	Whig	1849–50
13. Millard Fillmore	Whig	1850–53
14. Franklin Pierce	Democrat	1853–57
15. James Buchanan	Democrat	1857–61
16. Abraham Lincoln	Republican	1861–65
17. Andrew Johnson	Republican	1865–69
18. Ulysses S. Grant	Republican	1869–77
19. Rutherford B. Hayes	Republican	1877–81
20. James A. Garfield	Republican	1881
21. Chester A. Arthur	Republican	1881–85
22. Grover Cleveland	Democrat	1885–89
23. Benjamin Harrison	Republican	1889–93
24. Grover Cleveland	Democrat	1893–97
25. William McKinley	Republican	1897–1901

Name	Party	Date
26. Theodore Roosevelt	Republican	1901–9
27. William H. Taft	Republican	1909–13
28. Woodrow Wilson	Democrat	1913–21
29. Warren G. Harding	Republican	1921–23
30. Calvin Coolidge	Republican	1923–29
31. Herbert Hoover	Republican	1929–33
32. Franklin D. Roosevelt	Democrat	1933–45
33. Harry S. Truman	Democrat	1945–53
34. Dwight D. Eisenhower	Republican	1953–61
35. John F. Kennedy	Democrat	1961–63
36. Lyndon B. Johnson	Democrat	1963–69
37. Richard M. Nixon	Republican	1969–74
38. Gerald Rudolph Ford, Jr	Republican	1974–77
39. James Carter	Democrat	1977–

Early Roman Emperors

[Julius Caesar (Dictator)]	49–44 BC
Augustus	29 BC–AD 14
Tiberius	AD 14–37
Caligula	AD 37–41
Claudius	AD 41–54
Nero	AD 54–68
Galba	AD 68–69
Otho	AD 69
Vitellius	AD 69
Vespasian	AD 69–79
Titus	AD 79–81
Domitian	AD 81–96

(Only the first six were of the family of Julius.
Julius Caesar himself refused the Imperial Crown,
but nevertheless ruled as a dictator.)

English Kings and Queens

Sovereign	Date of Accession	Date of Death
SAXON		
Egbert	827	839
Ethelwulf	839	858
(Ethelbald	858)	860
(Ethelbert	858)	866
Ethelred	866	871
Alfred the Great	871	901
Edward the Elder	901	925
Athelstan	925	940
Edmund	940	946
Edred	946	955
Edwy	955	959
Edgar	959	975
Edward the Martyr	975	978
Ethelred II	978	1016
Edmund Ironside	1016	1016
DANISH		
Canute the Dane	1017	1035
Harold I	1035	1040
Hardicanute	1040	1042
SAXON		
Edward the Confessor	1042	1066
Harold II	1066	1066

Sovereign	Date of Accession	Date of Death
THE HOUSE OF NORMANDY		
William I	1066	1087
William II	1087	1100
Henry I	1100	1135
Stephen	1135	1154
THE HOUSE OF PLANTAGENET		
Henry II	1154	1189
Richard I	1189	1199
John	1199	1216
Henry III	1216	1272
Edward I	1272	1307
Edward II	1307	1327
Edward III	1327	1377
Richard II	1377	1400
		(Deposed 1399)
THE HOUSE OF LANCASTER		
Henry IV	1399	1413
Henry V	1413	1422
Henry VI	1422	1471
		(Deposed 1461)
THE HOUSE OF YORK		
Edward IV	1461	1483
Edward V	1483	1483
Richard III	1483	1485
THE HOUSE OF TUDOR		
Henry VII	1485	1509
Henry VIII	1509	1547
Edward VI	1547	1553
Jane*	1553	1554
Mary I	1553	1558
Elizabeth I	1558	1603

*Lady Jane Grey

British Kings and Queens

Sovereign	Date of Accession	Date of Death
THE HOUSE OF STUART		
James I (VI of Scotland)	1603	1625

Sovereign	Date of Accession		Date of Death
Charles I	1625	(Beheaded)	1649
Charles II	1649		1685

COMMONWEALTH DECLARED MAY 19TH, 1649
OLIVER CROMWELL, LORD PROTECTOR, 1653-8
RICHARD CROMWELL, LORD PROTECTOR, 1658-9

THE HOUSE OF STUART

James II (VII of Scotland)	1685	(Deposed 1688)	
William III and	1689		1702
Mary II	1689		1694
Anne	1702		1714

THE HOUSE OF HANOVER

George I	1714	1727
George II	1727	1760
George III	1760	1820
George IV	1820	1830
William IV	1830	1837
Victoria	1837	1901

THE HOUSE OF SAXE-COBURG

Edward VII	1901	1910

THE HOUSE OF WINDSOR

George V	1910	1936
Edward VIII	1936	1972
	(Abdicated 1936)	
George VI	1936	1952
Elizabeth II	1952	—

Scottish Kings and Queens

Sovereign	Date of Accession		Date of Death
Malcolm III (Canmore)	1057		1093
Donald Ban	1093		—
Duncan II	1094		1094
Donald Ban	(Restored) 1094		1097
Edgar	1097		1107
Alexander I	1107		1124
David I	1124		1153

Sovereign	Date of Accession	Date of Death
Malcolm IV (The Maiden)	1153	1165
William I (The Lion)	1165	1214
Alexander II	1214	1249
Alexander III	1249	1286
Margaret, Maid of Norway	1286	1290
John Baliol	1292	1296
Robert I (Bruce)	1306	1329
David II	1329	1371
Robert II (Stewart)	1371	1390
Robert III	1390	1406
James I	1406	1437
James II	1437	1460
James III	1460	1488
James IV	1488	1513
James V	1513	1542
Mary	1542	1587
James VI (Ascended the Throne of England, 1603)	1567	1625

HM Queen Elizabeth II

Her Majesty Queen Elizabeth II celebrates the Silver Jubilee of her accession to the throne on June 7th, 1977.

Notable Dates

Born – Elizabeth Alexandra Mary of Windsor	April 21st, 1926
Married – HRH The Prince Philip, Duke of Edinburgh	November 20th, 1947
HRH The Prince of Wale (Charles Philip Arthur George) born	November 14th, 1948
HRH Princess Anne Elizabeth Alice Louise born (married Captain Mark Anthony Peter Phillips November 14th, 1973)	August 15th, 1950
HM Queen Elizabeth acceded to the throne	February 6th, 1952
Coronation Day	June 2nd, 1953
HRH Prince Andrew Albert Christian Edward born	February 19th, 1960
HRH Prince Edward Antony Richard Louis born	March 10th, 1964

The British Orders of Chivalry

(In order of importance)

THE MOST NOBLE ORDER OF THE GARTER (1348) – KG.
  Generally confined to Royalty and Peers.

THE MOST ANCIENT AND MOST NOBLE ORDER OF THE THISTLE (1687) – KT.
  Confined to Royalty and Scottish nobles.

THE MOST ILLUSTRIOUS ORDER OF ST PATRICK (1783) – KP.
  Consists only of Her Majesty the Queen. There are no other members.

THE MOST HONOURABLE ORDER OF THE BATH (1725)
  The most important order of chivalry conferred on commoners. It has both civil and military divisions in three grades: 1st class, Knight Grand Cross (GCB); 2nd class, Knight Commander (KCB); 3rd class, Companion (CB).

THE ORDER OF MERIT (1902) – OM.
  Limited to 24 members. It has two divisions – civil and military.

THE MOST EXALTED ORDER OF THE STAR OF INDIA (1861)
  This Order has three classes – Knight Grand Commander (GCSI); Knight Commander (KCSI); and Companion (CSI). It has not been conferred since 1947 and is obsolescent.

THE MOST DISTINGUISHED ORDER OF ST MICHAEL AND ST GEORGE (1818)
  The usual reward for distinguished service in the British Empire and Commonwealth. The grades are Knight Grand Cross (GCMG); Knight Commander (KCMG) and Companion (CMG).

THE MOST EMINENT ORDER OF THE INDIAN EMPIRE (1877)
Has not been conferred since 1947 when India achieved independence.
There are three grades – Knight Grand Commander (GCIE); Knight
Commander (KCIE), and Companion (CIE).

THE ROYAL VICTORIAN ORDER (1896)
Awarded for service to the Royal Family. There are five classes – Knights
Grand Cross (GCVO), Knights Commander (KCVO), Commanders
(CVO), and Members (MVO). Women are admitted and a Dame
Commander uses the letters DCVO after her name.

THE MOST EXCELLENT ORDER OF THE BRITISH EMPIRE (1917)
There are five classes of member – Knights Grand Cross (GBE),
Knights Commander (KBE), Commanders (CBE), Officers (OBE)
and Members (MBE). A Dame Commander uses the letters DBE after
her name.

ORDER OF THE COMPANIONS OF HONOUR (1917) – CH.
Limited to sixty-five recipients.

THE KNIGHTS BACHELOR do not constitute a Royal Order – they
comprise the surviving representation of the ancient State Orders of
Knighthood.

Principal British Decorations and Medals

(In order of precedence)
The Victoria Cross (1856) – VC – 'For Valour'
The George Cross (1940) – GC – 'For Gallantry'
The Distinguished Service Order (1886) – DSO
British Orders of Knighthood
Royal Red Cross (1883) – RRC – For Ladies
Distinguished Service Cross (1914) – DSC
Military Cross (December 1914) – MC
Distinguished Flying Cross (1918) – DFC
Air Force Cross (1918) – AFC
Albert Medal (1866) – AM – 'For Gallantry in Saving Life at Sea' or
'on Land'
Medal for Distinguished Conduct in the Field (1854) – DCM
Conspicuous Gallantry Medal (1874) – CGM
The George Medal (1940) – GM
Distinguished Service Medal (1914) – DSM
Military Medal (1916) – MM
Distinguished Flying Medal (1918) – DFM
British Empire Medal (formerly the Medal of the Order of the British
Empire, for Meritorious Service) – BEM

British Flags

The word flag is of Germanic origin and was used in the 15th and 16th centuries to mean a piece of cloth or other material displaying the insignia of a community or armed force, an individual or an office. Flags were signs of leadership and were used originally mainly in warfare. They served to identify friend and foe, and were useful as rallying points. Flags of various forms are known as colours, standards, banners, ensigns, pennons, guidons and burgees.

THE UNION JACK, the national flag of the United Kingdom, was adopted after the Union of England and Scotland in 1606. The name is derived from the use of the Union Flag on the jack staff of naval vessels. It consists of the cross of St George, the patron saint of England (a red cross on a white field), the cross of St Andrew, patron saint of Scotland (a diagonal cross of saltire, white on a blue field), and a cross similar to that of St Patrick, patron saint of Ireland (a red saltire on a white field). The cross of St Patrick was added in 1801.

The Union Flag is hoisted on Government and Public buildings and, in London, on the occasion of the opening and closing of Parliament by the Queen, and from 8 AM to sunset on certain days as follows:

February 6th (1952) – Her Majesty's Accession
February 19th (1960) – Birthday of Prince Andrew
March 1st – St David's Day (in Wales only)
March 10th (1964) – Birthday of Prince Edward
April 21st (1926) – Birthday of Her Majesty the Queen

April 23rd – St George's Day (in England only)
June 2nd (1953) – Coronation Day
June 10th (1921) – Birthday of the Duke of Edinburgh
August 4th (1900) – Birthday of Her Majesty Queen Elizabeth the Queen Mother
August 15th (1950) – Birthday of Princess Anne
August 21st (1930) – Birthday of Princess Margaret
November 14th (1948) – Birthday of the Prince of Wales
November 20th (1947) – Her Majesty's Wedding Day
November 30th – St Andrew's Day (in Scotland only)
(also on the Queen's Official Birthday, June 11th, 1977, and Remembrance Sunday, November 13th, 1977)

THE ROYAL ARMS – displayed in banner form is mistakenly referred to as the Royal Standard. It is, in fact, a banner and is used as such – only being flown to indicate the presence of the Sovereign.

There are several versions of the Royal Arms – the Arms of the King of the Scots (still in use in Scotland); the Arms of Great Britain (as used officially in Scotland); and the Arms of Great Britain (as used officially in England). The present version of the form of the Royal Arms as used in England came into use in the reign of Queen Victoria. It is divided into four quarters. The 1st and 4th quarters contain the 3 lions *passant* of England; the 2nd quarter the lion *rampant* of Scotland and the 3rd quarter the harp of Ireland.

THE WHITE ENSIGN is the flag of the Royal Navy. A white flag bears the cross of St George with a small Union Jack in the top corner next to the flagstaff.

THE RED ENSIGN ('the Red Duster') is flown by all British merchant vessels not belonging to the Royal Navy. It is plain red, with a Union Jack in the top corner next to the flagstaff.

THE BLUE ENSIGN – similar to the Red Ensign but with a blue background – the flag of the Royal Naval Reserve.

The Union Flag and the White Ensign were worn at the Battle of Trafalgar in 1805 when Nelson hoisted his signal 'England expects that every man will do his duty'. In 1800 a code of flag-signals in which each of the hoists of flags meant a word, or even a letter, had been devised. It included a 'telegraph' flag, ten flags numbered from 1 to 9 and 0, and a substitute flag to repeat one already included in a hoist.

Nelson's hoists, a flag signal in code that became a watchword of the British Navy, were: the telegraph flag; 253; 269; 863; 261; 471; 958; 220, literally 2, substitute, 0; 370; and 4, 21, 19, 24 – the word duty, which was not in the vocabulary and had to be spelt out.

21 THE LAW

The Law

The Law, as we know it in England today, dates back to 1066, the year of the Norman Conquest, but it really began to take shape in the reign of Henry II (1154–89).

The sources of English law are:

1. Common Law – the oldest source of law in the English legal system. The unwritten law based on the practice and custom of the country developed and administered by judges in the courts. The common law is to be found embodied in 'case law' – the decisions of courts on cases throughout the centuries.
2. Statute Law – laws laid down by Act of Parliament, local by-laws, and Orders in Council (made by Ministers under authority of an Act of Parliament).

Reinforcing the common law to make up the body of English law are over 3,000 Acts of Parliament, and 300,000 reported cases. There are some 22,500 solicitors and 2,500 barristers.

Solicitors are the general practitioners of the legal profession. They draw up wills and conveyances for the transfer of property. They give advice on a whole range of problems and prepare cases for the High Court as well as acting as advocates themselves in magistrates' and county courts.

Barristers are the specialists of the legal profession and can only obtain clients through a solicitor. The barrister is usually described as 'counsel'.

A barrister wears wig and gown in the House of Lords, the High Court,

STRUCTURE OF THE CIVIL AND CRIMINAL COURTS IN ENGLAND AND WALES

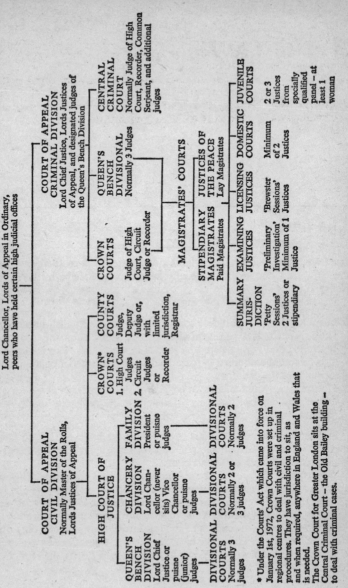

HOUSE OF LORDS
Lord Chancellor, Lords of Appeal in Ordinary,
peers who have held certain high judicial offices

**COURT OF APPEAL
CIVIL DIVISION**
Normally Master of the Rolls,
Lords Justices of Appeal

**COURT OF APPEAL
CRIMINAL DIVISION**
Lord Chief Justice, Lords Justices
of Appeal, and designated judges of
the Queen's Bench Division

**HIGH COURT OF
JUSTICE**

**QUEEN'S
BENCH
DIVISION**
Lord Chief
Justice or
puisne
(junior)
judges

**CHANCERY
DIVISION**
Lord Chan-
cellor (never
sits) Vice
Chancellor
or puisne
judges

**FAMILY
DIVISION**
President
or puisne
judges

**DIVISIONAL
COURTS**
Normally 3
judges

**DIVISIONAL
COURTS**
Normally 2 or
3 judges

**DIVISIONAL
COURTS**
Normally 2
judges

**CROWN*
COURTS**
1. High Court
   Judges
2. Circuit
   Judges or
   Recorder

**COUNTY
COURTS**
Judge,
Deputy
Judge or,
with
limited
jurisdiction,
Registrar

**CROWN
COURTS**
Judge of High
Court, Circuit
Judge or Recorder

**QUEEN'S
BENCH
DIVISIONAL
COURT**
Normally 3 Judges

**CENTRAL
CRIMINAL
COURT**
Normally Judge of High
Court, Recorder, Common
Serjeant, and additional
judges

MAGISTRATES' COURTS

**STIPENDIARY
MAGISTRATES**
Paid Magistrates

**JUSTICES OF
THE PEACE**
Lay Magistrates

**SUMMARY
JURIS-
DICTION**
'Petty
Sessions'
2 Justices or
stipendiary

**EXAMINING
JUSTICES**
'Preliminary
Investigation'
Minimum of 1
Justice

**LICENSING
JUSTICES**
'Brewster
Sessions'
3 Justices

**DOMESTIC
COURTS**
Minimum
of 2
Justices

**JUVENILE
COURTS**
2 or 3
Justices
from
specially
qualified
panel – at
least 1
woman

* Under the Courts' Act which came into force on
January 1st, 1972, Crown Courts were set up in
regional centres to deal with civil and criminal
procedures. They have jurisdiction to sit, as
and when required, anywhere in England and Wales that
is needed.
The Crown Court for Greater London sits at the
Central Criminal Court – the Old Bailey building –
to deal with criminal cases.

SPECIAL COURTS: Coroners' Courts, National Industrial Relations Court, Restrictive Practices Court at County Courts and at Courts Martial. A solicitor wears a gown but not a wig. Neither barristers nor solicitors wear gowns in Magistrates' Courts.

There are two main divisions of the Law:

1. **Civil Law** – concerning the maintenance of private claims and the redress of private wrongs; and
2. **Criminal Law** – dealing with offences that are deemed to harm the whole community, and thus to be an offence against the Sovereign.

A Table of Kindred and Affinity

Wherein whosoever are related are forbidden by the
Church of England to marry together

A man may not marry his:	*A woman may not marry her:*
Mother	Father
Daughter	Son
Father's mother	Father's father
Mother's mother	Mother's father
Son's daughter	Son's son
Daughter's daughter	Daughter's son
Sister	Brother
Father's daughter	Father's son
Mother's daughter	Mother's son
Wife's mother	Husband's father
Wife's daughter	Husband's son
Father's wife	Mother's husband
Son's wife	Daughter's husband
Father's father's wife	Father's mother's husband
Mother's father's wife	Mother's mother's husband
Wife's father's mother	Husband's father's father
Wife's mother's mother	Husband's mother's father
Wife's son's daughter	Husband's son's son
Wife's daughter's daughter	Husband's daughter's son
Son's son's wife	Son's daughter's husband
Daughter's son's wife	Daughter's daughter's husband
Father's sister	Father's brother

Religious Populations of the World

Religions	N. America*	S. America	Europe	Asia	Africa	Oceania†	World
Roman Catholic	126,468,000	147,219,000	226,303,000	47,622,000	28,751,000	4,107,000	580,470,000
Eastern Orthodox	3,675,000	47,000	114,103,000	2,819,000	4,956,000	84,000	125,684,000
Protestant	84,115,000	3,160,000	101,600,000	11,032,000	8,349,000	9,864,000	218,120,000
Total Christian:	214,258,000	150,426,000	442,006,000	61,473,000	42,056,000	14,055,000	924,274,000
Jewish	6,035,000	705,000	4,025,000	2,460,000	238,000	74,000	13,537,000
Muslim	166,000	416,000	13,848,000	374,167,000	104,297,000	118,000	493,012,000
Zoroastrian	—	—	12,000	126,000	—	—	138,000
Shinto	31,000	116,000	2,000	69,513,000	—	—	69,662,000
Taoist	16,000	19,000	12,000	54,277,000	—	—	54,324,000
Confucian	96,000	109,000	55,000	371,261,000	9,000	57,000	371,587,000
Buddhist	187,000	157,000	8,000	176,568,000	—	—	176,920,000
Hindu	55,000	660,000	160,000	434,447,000	1,205,000	218,000	436,745,000
TOTALS	220,844,000	152,608,000	460,128,000	1,544,292,000	147,805,000	14,522,000	2,540,199,000

* Includes Central America and the West Indies
† Includes New Zealand and Australia as well as islands of the South Pacific

A man may not marry his:	*A woman may not marry her*:
Mother's sister	Mother's brother
Brother's daughter	Brother's son
Sister's daughter	Sister's son

Patron Saints of the British Isles

'Why were the saints, saints? Because they were cheerful when it was difficult to be cheerful, patient when it was difficult to be patient; and because they pushed on when they wanted to stand still, and kept silent when they wanted to talk, and were agreeable when they wanted to be disagreeable. That was all. It was quite simple and always will be.'

(Anon.)

Each of the countries in the British Isles has its own patron saint.

St George is the patron saint of England, cavalrymen, chivalry and soldiers. He is believed to have been born of Christian parents at Cappadocia in the third century, and the most famous legend associated with him is the story of how he killed the dragon. He was made the patron saint of England in the reign of Edward III. His white banner with its red cross forms the basis of the Union Jack. His feast day is on April 23rd. *Emblems:* Knight with dragon. Red cross on shield or banner.

St Andrew, patron saint of Scotland, Russia and golfers, was born at Bethsaida on the Lake of Galilee and lived at Capernaum. He was a fisherman, one of the Twelve Apostles and the brother of St Peter. His annual festival is observed on November 30th. *Emblems:* Transverse cross. Fishing net.

St David is the patron saint of Wales. His Day is observed on March 1st, supposedly the anniversary of his death. He was the son of a prince, became a hermit and founded a monastery. He became Bishop of Menevia, and when he died the name of Menevia was changed to St David's, and it is there in Pembrokeshire that the great Welsh Cathedral of St David's still stands. *Emblem:* Dove on shoulder.

St Patrick is the patron saint of Ireland. There are so many conflicting stories about Patrick of Ireland that some scholars think there may have been two Patricks. But legends gravitate towards one great commanding figure named Magnus Sucatus Patricus, who was born in England about 389. Patrick was captured by pirates when he was sixteen years old and sold as a slave in Northern Ireland. He escaped, was ordained, returned to Ireland as a missionary and converted the country to Christianity. That was in 432. It is thought he died either in 461 or 493. His feast day is celebrated on March 17th.
Emblems: Bishop with serpents. Shamrock.

Patron Saints of the Arts, Trades and Professions

Air Hostesses	St Bona	Housewives	St Martha
Animals	St Roch	Lawyers	St Yvo
Architects	St Thomas	Lovers	St Valentine
Artists	St Luke	Musicians	St Cecilia
Bakers	St Honorius	Painters	St Luke and
Barbers	St Cosmas		St Lazarus
Bee Keepers	St Bartholomew	Preachers	St Paul
Beggars	St Martin	Queens	St Elizabeth of
Bookbinders	St John the Evangelist	Scholars	Hungary St Catherine
Cab-drivers	St Fiacre	Shoemakers	St Crispin
Careless People	St Anthony of Padua	Thieves	St Nicholas
Cooks	St Laurence	Toothache Sufferers	St Apollonia
Fishermen	St Peter	Travellers	St Christopher
Fishmongers	St Magnus		

The Books of the Old Testament

Genesis	Joshua	1 Kings
Exodus	Judges	2 Kings
Leviticus	Ruth	1 Chronicles
Numbers	1 Samuel	2 Chronicles
Deuteronomy	2 Samuel	Ezra

Nehemiah	Jeremiah	Jonah
Esther	Lamentations	Micah
Job	Ezekiel	Nahum
Psalms	Daniel	Habakkuk
Proverbs	Hosea	Zephaniah
Ecclesiastes	Joel	Haggai
Song of Solomon	Amos	Zechariah
Isaiah	Obadiah	Malachi

The Books of the New Testament

Matthew	Ephesians	Hebrews
Mark	Philippians	James
Luke	Colossians	1 Peter
John	1 Thessalonians	2 Peter
The Acts	2 Thessalonians	1 John
Romans	1 Timothy	2 John
1 Corinthians	2 Timothy	3 John
2 Corinthians	Titus	Jude
Galatians	Philemon	Revelation

The Ten Commandments

1. You shall have no other god to set against me.
2. You shall not make a carved image for yourself nor the likeness of anything in the heavens above, or on the earth below, or in the waters under the earth. You shall not bow down to them or worship them; for I, the LORD your God, am a jealous god. I punish the children for the sins of the fathers to the third and fourth generations of those who hate me. But I keep faith with thousands, with those who love me and keep my commandments.
3. You shall not make wrong use of the name of the LORD your God; the LORD will not leave unpunished the man who misuses his name.
4. Keep the sabbath day holy as the LORD your God commanded you. You have six days to labour and do all your work. But the seventh day is a sabbath of the LORD your God; that day you shall not do any work, neither you, your son or your daughter, your slave or your slave-girl, your ox, your ass, or any of your cattle, nor the alien

within your gates, so that your slaves and slave-girls may rest as you do. Remember that you were slaves in Egypt and the LORD your God brought you out with a strong hand and an outstretched arm, and for that reason the LORD your God commanded you to keep the sabbath day.

5. Honour your father and your mother, as the LORD your God commanded you, so that you may live long, and that it may be well with you in the land which the LORD your God is giving you.

6. You shall not commit murder.

7. You shall not commit adultery.

8. You shall not steal.

9. You shall not give false evidence against your neighbour.

10. You shall not covet your neighbour's wife; you shall not set your heart on your neighbour's house, his land, his slave, his slave-girl, his ox, his ass, or on anything that belongs to him.

The United Bible Societies have issued at least one book of the Bible in 1,577 languages and dialects.

23 BRITISH HALLMARKS ON GOLD AND SILVER WARES

British Hallmarks on Gold and Silver Wares

Hallmarks are symbols stamped on articles of gold or silver to indicate that they have been accurately tested, or assayed, and that the precious metal conforms to one of the legal standards of purity.

Hall-marking was instituted by a statute of King Edward I in 1300. In London it is the responsibility of the Worshipful Company of Goldsmiths. The London Assay Office is at Goldsmiths' Hall and this is the origin of the word 'hallmark'.

A hallmark usually consists of four symbols – the Maker's Mark, the Standard Mark, the Assay Office Mark and the Date Letter.

The Maker's Mark was instituted in 1363 by statute of King Edward III. It originally took the form of an emblem, a bell, a bird or a *fleur-de-lys* connected with the name of the maker or the shops where he worked. Nowadays it consists of the initials of the Christian and surname of the person or firm submitting the article to the Assay Office.

It takes the form of the symbol NM in the example overleaf.

The Standard Mark was introduced by the Goldsmiths' Company in 1544. It denotes the minimum gold or silver content. The current legal standards and their marks are shown overleaf.

The Assay Office Mark shows which Assay Office tested the article. There were formerly assay offices in other towns – Chester, Exeter, Glasgow, Newcastle, Norwich and York – each with its own distinguishing mark. The existing Assay Offices are at London, Birmingham, Sheffield, and Edinburgh and their distinguishing marks are shown overleaf.

The Date Letter denotes the year in which the article was hallmarked. It differs at the various assay offices. The date letter is changed at the London office in May each year, in July at Birmingham and Sheffield, and at Edinburgh in October.

It consists of a shield enclosing a letter of the alphabet.

	MARK	STANDARD	MINIMUM PERCENTAGE			
NM MAKERS MARK						
		Sterling silver Marked in England	92.5		London	Sterling silver & gold
		Sterling silver Marked in Scotland	92.5		London	Britannia silver
		Britannia silver	95.84		Birmingham	silver & gold
	22	22 carat gold Marked in England	91.66		Sheffield	silver
	18	18 carat gold Marked in England	75.0		Sheffield	gold
	14 ·585	14 carat gold	58.5		Edinburgh	silver & gold
	9 375	9 carat gold	37.5			

A. Music

Popular Music

The 'pop' music industry has grown to enormous proportions since the end of the Second World War.

In 1954 two important events took place in the world of popular music in the United States. The first was that Bill (William John Clifton) Haley launched a group called The Comets. Sales of their top-selling pop record *Rock around the Clock*, made on April 12th, 1954, are said to have reached 25,000,000.

The second was that Elvis Presley made some recordings in a somewhat similar style – and without Presley there would be no 'pop' as we know it today. The age of 'Rock and Roll' had begun. Towards the end of the Fifties Traditional Jazz was popular, followed a decade later by Rhythm and Blues and still later by Soul Music. Progressive pop arose out of the attempts in the Sixties to link popular music with, for example, the classical arrangement of music, the Indian sitar, and so on.

The first record to sell a million copies was the aria 'Vesti la giubba' ('On with the motley') from Leoncavallo's opera *I Pagliacci*, sung by Enrico Caruso, and first recorded, with piano accompaniment, on November 12th, 1902.

The first actual golden disc was one sprayed by RCA Victor and presented to US trombonist and bandleader Glenn Miller for *Chattanooga Choo Choo* on February 10th, 1942.

Elvis Presley claims to have more Golden Discs than any other individual. He is said to have twenty-eight. The most as a group have gone to the Beatles, who have thirty-eight, with eight more awards each to individual members of the group.

Some records have won two Golden Discs – like the LP *Blue Hawaii* – not forgetting the fantastic *Don't Be Cruel*.

The only audited measure of million-selling discs within the United States is certification by the Recording Industry of America (RIAA), which began in 1958.

The Beatles' record *With the Beatles* was the first British LP to sell 1,000,000 copies and their *I Want to Hold Your Hand* is the top-selling British record of all time. It was released in 1963 and had achieved world sales of over 13,000,000 by January 1975.

In their first tour of the United States the Beatles grossed $19,000,000 and for one performance in the USA they received a fee of $189,000 (then £67,500) – the highest fee ever paid to recording artists for a single performance.

The Beatles' first single, *Love Me Do*, was released on October 5th, 1962. The last record they made together as a group was *Let It Be* in 1970. In the week ending March 21st, 1964, they were Nos. 1, 2, 3, 4 and 5 in the US chart with *Twist and Shout, Can't Buy Me Love, She Loves You, I Want to Hold Your Hand* and *Please Please Me*: and Nos. 1 and 2 on the LP charts with *Meet the Beatles* and *Introducing the Beatles*.

Sales of the double (4-sided) British LP *Jesus Christ Superstar*, by Andrew Lloyd Webber and Tim Rice, released on October 10th, 1970, have topped the six million mark.

The best-selling LP is the 20th Century Fox album *Sing We Now of Christmas*, issued in 1958. In 1963 this title was changed to *The Little Drummer Boy* and by November 1972 estimated sales were more than 14,000,000.

The all-time best-seller among LP's of musical film shows is the sound-track album of *The Sound of Music*, released in 1965.

Irving Berlin's record *White Christmas*, first recorded in 1941, has sold more copies than any other gramophone record. By December 1974 sales had reached an estimated total of 135,000,000.

The songs most frequently sung in English are: *Happy Birthday to You* (sung in space by the American astronauts on their 1969 Apollo mission), *For He's a Jolly Good Fellow* and *Auld Lang Syne*.

Amazing Grace, a 200-year old Scottish hymn, recorded by the Band of the Royal Scots Dragoon Guards, was played for the first time on the BBC's 'Late Night Extra' programme on January 11th, 1972. Within three weeks of its release it became No. 1 in the charts.

In November 1974, a unique silent LP was released. It was 'recorded' by

Jerry Cammarata of Staten Island, New York, and runs for 52 minutes 10 seconds.

The song with the longest title? Hoagy Carmichael's *I'm a Cranky Old Yank in a Clanky Old Tank on the Streets of Yokohama with my Honolulu Mama Doin' those Beat-o, Beat-o, Flat-on-My-Seat-o, Hirohito Blues.*

Record sales continue to increase. Singles and albums reached a sales figure of £141 million in 1975 compared with £115·5 million in 1974. Cassettes now account for 15–20 per cent of the UK market, and sales of tapes and records have dropped in the past year.

Television advertising is now being used to sell compilation albums. First in this field, in 1972, was K-Tel with '20 Dynamic Hits' which sold 750,000 records.

Soul and Reggae music head the popularity lists with the disco sounds, now heard in clubs and pubs all over the country.

Great Composers

Henry Purcell (1659–95) English
George Friederich Handel (1685–1759) German
Johann Sebastian Bach (1685–1750) German
Franz Joseph Hadyn (1732–1809) Austrian
Wolfgang Amadeus Mozart (1756–1791) Austrian
Ludwig Van Beethoven (1770–1827) German
Gioacchino Rossini (1792–1868) Italian
Franz Peter Schubert (1797–1828) Austrian
Gaetano Donizetti (1797–1848) Italian
Vincenzo Bellini (1801–1835) Italian
Hector Berlioz (1803–1869) French
Mikhail Ivanovitch Glinka (1804–1857) Russian
Frédéric Chopin (1810–1849) Polish
Robert Schumann (1810–1856) German
Franz Liszt (1811–1886) Hungarian
Richard Wagner (1813–1883) German
Giuseppe Verdi (1813–1901) Italian
Charles Gounod (1818–1893) French
Jacques Offenbach (1819–1880) German
César Franck (1822–1890) Belgian
Anton Bruckner (1824–1896) Austrian
Johannes Brahms (1833–1897) German
Alexander Borodin (1833–1887) Russian
Georges Bizet (1838–1875) French
Modest Petrovitch Mussorgsky (1839–1881) Russian

Peter Ilyich Tchaikovsky (1840–1893) Russian
Antonin Dvorak (1841–1904) Czechoslovakian
Arthur Sullivan (1842–1900) English
Nicolai Andreyevitch Rimsky-Korsakov (1844–1908) Russian
Edward Elgar (1857–1934) English
Giacomo Puccini (1858–1924) Italian
Gustav Mahler (1860–1911) Austrian
Claude Debussy (1862–1918) French
Frederick Delius (1862–1934) British
Richard Strauss (1864–1949) German
Ralph Vaughan Williams (1872–1958) English
Serge Rachmaninov (1873–1943) Russian
Gustav Holst (1874–1934) English
Arnold Schoenberg (1874–1951) Austrian
Maurice Ravel (1875–1937) French
Béla Bartók (1881–1945) Hungarian
Igor Fedorovitch Stravinsky (1882–1971) Russian
Serge Prokofiev (1891–1953) Russian
Paul Hindemith (1895–1963) German
Jean Sibelius (1865–1957) Finnish
Kurt Weill (1900–1950) German
Benjamin Britten (1913–1976) English
Aaron Copland (1900–   ) American
William Walton (1902–   ) English
Michael Tippett (1905–   ) English

Principal Instruments of the Symphony Orchestra

Strings	*Woodwind*
Violin	Flute
Viola	Piccolo
Cello	Oboe
Double Bass	Cor Anglais
Harp	Clarinet
	Bass Clarinet
	Bassoon
	Contra Bassoon

Brass
Horn
Trumpet
Trombone
Tuba

Percussion
Timpani (or Kettle Drums)
Side Drum
Bass Drum
Cymbals
Triangle
Xylophone
Glockenspiel

Some Musical Terms and their Meanings

ADAGIO – very slow
AGITATO – excited
ALLEGRO – cheerful, lively
ANDANTE – quiet, peaceful tempo
BARITONE – male voice between tenor and bass
BASS – deep-sounding; the lowest part in music
CONTRALTO – lowest register of the female voice
CRESCENDO – increasing the loudness gradually
DIMINUENDO – decreasing the loudness gradually
DOLCE – Sweet
FALSETTO – highest register of the voice as used by male altos
FORTE – loud, strong
FORTISSIMO – very loud
HEAD-VOICE – the highest register of the human voice
LACRIMOSO – tearfully
LARGO – in slow, dignified style
MEZZO SOPRANO – female voice, between soprano and contralto
MODERATO – at a moderate pace
PIANISSIMO – very soft
PRESTO – fast
RECITATIVE – declamatory singing, free in tempo and rhythm
REPRISE – repeat
RHYTHM – measured time
SOLO – alone
SOPRANO – the highest female voice
SOTTO – below, beneath
SPIRITUOSO – spirited
TENOR – the highest natural male voice
TIMBRE – quality of tone
VIRTUOSO – performer of exceptional skill

B. Painting

I. RENAISSANCE AND MANNERIST PAINTING

(14th–16th centuries)
    Giotto di Bondone (1266–1337), Italian
    Sandro Botticelli (1441–1510), Florentine
    Leonardo da Vinci (1452–1519), Italian
    Michelangelo (1475–1564), Italian
    Raphael (1483–1520), Italian
    Albrecht Dürer (1471–1528), German
    Hans Holbein (1497–1543), German
    Giorgione (c1478–1510), Venetian
    Titian (1487–1576), Venetian
    El Greco (1541–1614), Spanish

II. BAROQUE THROUGH IMPRESSIONIST PAINTING

(17th–19th centuries)

FLANDERS
    Peter Paul Rubens (1577–1640)
    Anthony van Dyck (1599–1641)

THE NETHERLANDS
    Jan Vermeer (1632–1675)
    Frans Hals (?1580–1666)
    Rembrandt (1606–1669)

SPAIN
    Velasquez (1599–1660)
    Murillo (1617–1682)
    Goya (1746–1828)

FRANCE (17th and 18th centuries)
    Antoine Watteau (1684–1721)
    Jean Honoré Fragonard (1732–1806)
    Jacques Louis David (1748–1825)

ENGLAND
    William Hogarth (1697–1764)
    Sir Joshua Reynolds (1723–1792)
    Thomas Gainsborough (1727–1788)

William Blake (1757–1827)
John Constable (1776–1837)
Joseph Turner (1775–1851)
George Romney (1734–1802)

PRE-RAPHAELITES
Ford Madox Brown (1821–1893)
Dante Gabriel Rossetti (1828–1882)
William Holman Hunt (1827–1910)
Sir John Millais (1829–1896)
Sir Edward Burne-Jones (1833–1898)

FRANCE (19th century)
Jean Auguste Dominique Ingres (1780–1867)
Eugène Delacroix (1798–1863)
Jean Corot (1796–1875)
Honoré Daumier (1808–1879)
Édouard Manet (1832–1883)

THE IMPRESSIONISTS
Claude Monet (1840–1926)
Pierre Auguste Renoir (1841–1919)
Degas (1834–1917)

III. MODERN PAINTING (late 19th and 20th centuries)

POST IMPRESSIONISM
Toulouse-Lautrec (1864–1901), French
Vincent van Gogh (1853–1890), Dutch
Paul Gauguin (1848–1903), French
Paul Cézanne (1839–1906), French

FAUVISM
Henri Matisse (1869–1954), French
Raoul Dufy (1877–1953), French

CUBISM
Georges Braque (1882–1963), French
Juan Gris (1887–1927), Spanish
Pablo Picasso (1881–1973), Spanish

SURREALISM
Salvador Dali (1905–   ), Spanish

SOME WELL-KNOWN BRITISH PAINTERS OF TODAY

Victor Pasmore	Bridget Riley	L. S. Lowry
David Hockney	Ben Nicholson	Mark Tobey
Graham Sutherland	Alan Davie	John Bratby
William Scott	Sidney Nolan	Ceri Richards
Francis Bacon	Peter Blake	Bernard Cohen
Lucian Freud		

POP ART

Pop art appeared in England in the late 1950s and in America ten years later.

The highest price paid for an item of Pop Art was for 'Soup Can' by Andy Warhol. The 72″ × 54″ work was sold in May 1970 for £25,000.

C. Literature

Some Famous British Authors

		Best-known work
Daniel Defoe	1661 ?–1731	*Robinson Crusoe*
Sir Walter Scott	1771–1832	The *Waverley* novels
Jane Austen	1775–1817	*Pride and Prejudice*
Elizabeth Cleghorn Gaskell	1810–1865	*Cranford*
Frederick Marryat	1792–1848	*The Children of the New Forest*
William Makepeace Thackeray	1811–1863	*Vanity Fair*
Charles Dickens	1812–1870	*David Copperfield*
Charles Reade	1814–1884	*The Cloister and the Hearth*
Anthony Trollope	1815–1882	*The Warden*
Charlotte Brontë	1816–1855	*Jane Eyre*
Emily Brontë	1818–1848	*Wuthering Heights*
George Eliot (Mary Ann Evans)	1819–1880	*The Mill on the Floss*
Charles Kingsley	1819–1875	*The Water Babies*
Wilkie Collins	1824–1889	*The Moonstone*
Lord Lytton	1831–1891	*The Last Days of Pompeii*
Samuel Butler	1835–1902	*The Way of All Flesh*
Thomas Hardy	1840–1928	*Tess of the D'Urbervilles*

		Best-known work
Henry James	1843–1916	*The Turn of the Screw*
Joseph Conrad	1857–1924	*Lord Jim*
Sir A. Conan Doyle	1859–1930	*The Hound of the Baskervilles*
W. W. Jacobs	1863–1943	*The Monkey's Paw* (and other short stories)
Rudyard Kipling	1865–1936	*The Jungle Book*
H. G. Wells	1866–1946	*Kipps*
Arnold Bennett	1867–1931	*The Old Wives' Tale*
John Galsworthy	1869–1933	*The Forsyte Saga*
Hilaire Belloc	1870–1953	*Cautionary Tales*
G. K. Chesterton	1874–1936	The *Father Brown* stories
John Buchan	1875–1940	*The Thirty-Nine Steps*
D. H. Lawrence	1885–1930	*Sons and Lovers*
George Orwell	1903–1950	*Animal Farm*

Some Famous English Essayists

Francis Bacon	1561–1626	Robert Lynd	1879–1949
Joseph Addison	1672–1719	A. A. Milne	1882–1956
Oliver Goldsmith	1728–1774	Harold Nicolson	1886–1968
Charles Lamb	1775–1834	Neville Cardus	1889–1975
William Hazlitt	1778–1830	J. B. Priestley	1894–
Leigh Hunt	1784–1859	Aldous Huxley	1894–1963
Robert Louis Stevenson	1850–1894	Ian Mackay	1898–1952
E. V. Lucas	1868–1938	V. S. Pritchett	1900–

Some Famous British Poets

		Best-known work
William Langland	1330?–1400?	Piers Plowman
Geoffrey Chaucer	1340?–1400	The Canterbury Tales
Edmund Spenser	1552?–1599	Faerie Queene
Michael Drayton	1563–1631	The Ballad of Agincourt
John Milton	1608–1674	Paradise Lost
Samuel Butler	1612–1680	Hudibras
Alexander Pope	1688–1744	Rape of the Lock
Thomas Gray	1716–1771	Elegy in a Country Churchyard

		Best-known work
William Cowper	1731–1800	The Task
William Blake	1757–1828	Songs of Innocence and Songs of Experience
Robert Burns	1759–1796	Tam o'Shanter
William Wordsworth	1770–1850	Lyrical Ballads
Samuel Taylor Coleridge	1772–1834	Rime of the Ancient Mariner
Lord Byron	1788–1824	Don Juan
Percy Bysshe Shelley	1792–1822	Ode to the West Wind
John Keats	1795–1821	Endymion
Thomas Hood	1799–1845	Song of a Shirt
Elizabeth Barrett Browning	1806–1861	Sonnets from the Portuguese
Edward Fitzgerald	1809–1893	Rubaiyat of Omar Khayyam
Alfred Lord Tennyson	1809–1892	Idylls of the King
Robert Browning	1812–1889	The Pied Piper of Hamelin
Edward Lear	1812–1888	The Owl and the Pussycat
Christina Rossetti	1830–1894	Goblin Market
Robert Bridges	1844–1930	Testament of Beauty
A. E. Housman	1859–1936	A Shropshire Lad
Walter de la Mare	1873–1956	The Traveller
John Masefield	1876–1967	Sea Fever
T. S. Eliot	1888–1965	The Waste Land
Dylan Thomas	1914–1953	Under Milk Wood

The Poets Laureate

The origins of the office of Poet Laureate go back even before the time of Chaucer. Henry III ordered the payment of ten pounds to Henri d'Avranches, his 'official' poet, and the first holder of the title of *Versificator Regis* (the King's Versifier). From this stemmed the title and post of Poet Laureate as we know it today.

The first traditional poet laureate was Ben Jonson, who was granted a pension in recognition of his services as a poet, by James I in 1616. When he died the laurel crown passed to:

Sir William D'Avenant	1637
John Dryden	1670
Thomas Shadwell	1688

Nahum Tate	1692
Nicholas Rowe	1715
Rev. Laurence Eusden	1718
Colley Cibber	1730
William Whitehead	1757
Rev. Thomas Warton	1785
Henry James Pye	1790
Robert Southey	1813
William Wordsworth	1843
Lord Tennyson	1850
Alfred Austin	1896
Robert Bridges	1913
John Masefield	1930
Cecil Day-Lewis	1967
Sir John Betjeman	1972

The Works of William Shakespeare

	Date Written
Henry VI, Part I	1591
Henry VI, Part II	1591
Henry VI, Part III	1591
The Comedy of Errors	1592
Richard III	1593
Titus Andronicus	1593
The Taming of the Shrew	1594
The Two Gentlemen of Verona	1594
Love's Labour's Lost	1594
Romeo and Juliet	1595
Richard II	1595
A Midsummer Night's Dream	1596
King John	1596
The Merchant of Venice	1596
Henry IV, Part I	1597
Henry IV, Part II	1598
The Merry Wives of Windsor	1598
Much Ado About Nothing	1598
Henry V	1599

	Date Written
Julius Caesar	1599
As You Like It	1600
Twelfth Night	1601
Hamlet	1601
Troilus and Cressida	1602
All's Well That Ends Well	1603
Measure for Measure	1604
Othello	1604
King Lear	1605
Macbeth	1606
Antony and Cleopatra	1607
Pericles	1608
Coriolanus	1609
Timon of Athens	1609
Cymbeline	1610
The Winter's Tale	1611
The Tempest	1611
Henry VIII	1613
Venus and Adonis	1592
The Rape of Lucrece	1593
The Sonnets	

British Newspapers

Publication	Average net sales per publishing day: period Jan 1st–June 30th, 1976*
NATIONAL MORNINGS	
Daily Mirror	3,837,091
Sun	3,638,479
Daily Express (National)	2,607,785
Daily Mail	1,738,632
Daily Telegraph	1,315,473
Times	312,379
Guardian	308,700
Financial Times	176,649
Sporting Life	86,926
Sporting Chronicle	65,382

Publication	Average net sales per publishing day: period Jan 1st–June 30th, 1976*
NATIONAL SUNDAYS	
News of the World	5,162,136
Sunday Mirror	4,078,259
Sunday People	4,076,634
Sunday Express	3,436,209
Sunday Times	1,374,759
Sunday Telegraph	733,225
Observer	677,504
LONDON EVENINGS	
Evening News (Mon–Fri)	574,077
Evening News (Sat edn)	558,048
Evening Standard	431,094

Ten 'Bestselling' Consumer Magazines in Britain

Publication	Average net sales per publishing day: period Jan 1st–June 30th, 1976*
1. Woman's Weekly	1,645,417
2. Woman's Own	1,539,490
3. Woman	1,531,811
4. Family Circle	840,608
5. Woman's Realm	798,129
6. Weekend	791,803
7. Woman & Home	646,706
8. Living	607,228
9. Reveille	552,165
10. Titbits	451,610
Radio Times	3,490,324
TV Times	3,310,279

*Audit Bureau of Circulation

Some Alphabets

HEBREW

שרקצפעסנמלכיטחזוהדגבא

CYRILLIC

АБВГДЕЖЗИЙКЛМНОПР
СТУФХЦЧШЩЪЫЬЭЮЯ

ARABIC

ظظغغغفت ق ققف ك ك ك ك ك ك ل لل م مم ن

علی گی گی فی می س مبم ۱۲۳٤٥٦٧٨٩۰()؛:ﺳﺳﺎﻟ

GREEK

ΑΒΓΔΕΖΗΘΙΚΛΜΝΞΟΠΡΣΤΥΦΧΨΩ

Roman Numerals

1 ... I	12 ... XII	50 ... L	700 ... DCC
2 ... II	13 ... XIII	60 ... LX	800 ... DCCC
3 ... III	14 ... XIV	70 ... LXX	900 ... CM
4 ... IV	15 ... XV	80 ... LXXX	1000 ... M
5 ... V	16 ... XVI	90 ... XC	1500 ... MD
6 ... VI	17 ... XVII	100 ... C	1700 ... MDCC
7 ... VII	18 ... XVIII	200 ... CC	1800 ... MDCCC
8 ... VIII	19 ... XIX	300 ... CCC	1895 ... MDCCCXCV
9 ... IX	20 ... XX	400 ... CD	1900 ... MCM
10 ... X	30 ... XXX	500 ... D	1944 ... MCMXLIV
11 ... XI	40 ... XL	600 ... DC	2000 ... MM

A line placed over a numeral multiplies the number by 1,000, e.g.:
6,000 ... V̄I; 16,000 ... X̄VI; 160,000 ... C̄LX; 666,000 ... D̄C̄L̄X̄VI

Some Abbreviations in Common Use

A.D.	*Anno Domini* – in the year of our Lord	
Ad lib.	*Ad libitum* – to the extent desired	
A.M.	*Ante meridiem* – before noon	
A.M.	*Anno mundi* – in the year of the world	
A.M.D.G.	*Ad majorem Dei Gloriam* – to the greater glory of God	
c.	*circa* – about	
del.	*delineavit* – he (she) drew it	
D.G.	*Dei gratia* – by the Grace of God	
D.V.	*Deo volente* – God willing	
e.g.	*exempli gratia* – for the sake of example	
et al.	*et alia* – and others	
etc.	*et cetera* – and the other things	
et seq.	*et sequentia* – and the following	
ex lib.	*ex libris* – from the books of	
F.D.	*Fidei Defensor* – Defender of the Faith	
Fec.	*fecit* – he did it (or made it)	
fl.	*floruit* – he, or she, flourished	
ibid.	*ibidem* – in the same place	
i.e.	*id est* – that is	
i.q.	*idem quod* – the same as	
In loc.	*in loco* – in its place	
loc. cit.	*loco citato* – in the place mentioned	
N.B.	*Nota bene* – note well	
Nem. con.	*Nemine contradicente* – no-one contradicting	
No.	*Numero* – number	
Non seq.	*non sequitur* – it does not follow	
op. cit.	*opere citato* – in the work cited	
P.M.	*post meridiem* – after noon	
p.p.	(or *per pro.*) *per procurationem* – by proxy	
P.P.C.	*pour prendre congé* – to take leave	
Pro tem.	*pro tempore* – for the time being	
Prox.	*proximo* – next month	
P.S.	*Post Scriptum* – Postscript	
Q.e.d.	*quod erat demonstrandum* – which was to be proved	
q.e.f.	*quod erat faciendum* – which was to be done	
q.v.	*quod vide* – 'which see'	
Ro.	*recto* – on the right-hand page	
R.S.V.P.	*Répondez, s'il vous plaît* – answer, if you please	
Sic	so written	

S.P.Q.R.	*Senatus Populusque Romanus* – the Senate and People of Rome
Stet	Let it stand
Ult.	*ultimo* – in the preceding month
v.	*versus* – against
Verb. sap.	*Verbum sapienti satis est* – a word to the wise is enough
Viz.	*videlicet* – namely
Vo.	*verso* – on the left-hand page